William Shakespeare's

Timon of Athens
In Plain and Simple English

BookCaps Study Guides
www.bookcaps.com

Table of Contents

About This Series

The "Classic Retold" series started as a way of telling classics for the modern reader—being careful to preserve the themes and integrity of the original. Whether you want to understand Shakespeare a little more or are trying to get a better grasps of the Greek classics, there is a book waiting for you!

The series is expanding every month. Visit BookCaps.com to see all the books in the series, and while you are there join the Facebook page, so you are first to know when a new book comes out.

Characters

TIMON, a noble Athenian

LUCIUS LUCULLUS flattering Lords

SEMPRONIUS

VENTIDIUS, one of Timon's false Friends

APEMANTUS, a churlish Philosopher

ALCIBIADES, an Athenian Captain

FLAVIUS, Steward to Timon

FLAMINIUS LUCILIUS Servants to Timon

SERVILIUS

CAPHIS PHILOTUS Servants to Timon's Creditors

TITUS HORTENSIUS

Servants of Ventidius, and of Varro and Isidore (two of Timon's Creditor's)

THREE STRANGERS

AN OLD ATHENIAN

A PAGE

A FOOL

Poet, Painter, Jeweller, and Merchant.

PHRYNIA Mistresses to Alcibiades

TIMANDRA

Lords, Senators, Officers, Soldiers, Servants, Thieves, and Attendants

CUPID and Amazons in the Masque

Scene.--Athens, and the neighbouring Woods.

Comparative Version

Act 1

SCENE I. Athens. A hall in Timon's house.

Enter Poet, Painter, Jeweller, Merchant, and others, at several doors

Poet
Good day, sir.

Good day, sir.

Painter
I am glad you're well.

I'm glad you're well.

Poet
I have not seen you long: how goes the world?

I haven't seen you for a long time: how's life?

Painter
It wears, sir, as it grows.

It wears out sir, as it goes on.

Poet
Ay, that's well known:
But what particular rarity? what strange,
Which manifold record not matches? See,
Magic of bounty! all these spirits thy power
Hath conjured to attend. I know the merchant.

*Yes, that's well known:
But what particular unusual things are going
on? What unique things, never recorded
before? Look, generosity is as powerful as any
magician! Your power has brought all these
people here. I know that merchant.*

Painter
I know them both; th' other's a jeweller.

I know both of them, the other's a jeweller.

Merchant
O, 'tis a worthy lord.

Oh, that's a good lord.

Jeweller
Nay, that's most fix'd.

That's for sure.

Merchant
A most incomparable man, breathed, as it were,
To an untirable and continuate goodness:
He passes.

*An incomparable man, trained, as it were,
To have an unflagging and habitual goodness;
He beats everyone.*

Jeweller
I have a jewel here—

I have a jewel here-

Merchant
O, pray, let's see't: for the Lord Timon, sir?

*Oh, please let me see it. Is this for Lord Timon,
sir?*

Jeweller
If he will touch the estimate: but, for that—

If he'll pay the price I want: but, as to that-

Poet

[Reciting to himself] 'When we for recompense have
praised the vile,
It stains the glory in that happy verse
Which aptly sings the good.'

'When we praise the vile in return for payment,
it cheapens the value of the fine verse
which rightly praises the good.'

Merchant

'Tis a good form.

It's nicely cut.

Looking at the jewel

Jeweller

And rich: here is a water, look ye.

And rich: it's got a great shine to it, you can
see.

Painter

You are rapt, sir, in some work, some dedication
To the great lord.

You are involved, sir, in some work, something
In praise of the great lord.

Poet

A thing slipp'd idly from me.
Our poesy is as a gum, which oozes
From whence 'tis nourish'd: the fire i' the flint
Shows not till it be struck; our gentle flame
Provokes itself and like the current flies
Each bound it chafes. What have you there?

Something that just slipped out.
Poetry is like gum, which oozes
Out from its mother plant: the fire held
Within flint doesn't show until it's struck;
Our inspiration doesn't need any stimulus;
It starts itself and spreads everywhere like
A tide. What have you there?

Painter

A picture, sir. When comes your book forth?

A picture, sir. When's your book out?

Poet

Upon the heels of my presentment, sir.
Let's see your piece.

As soon as I give it to my lord, sir.
Let's see your piece.

Painter

'Tis a good piece.

It's a good piece.

Poet

So 'tis: this comes off well and excellent.

Yes it is: this is very well executed.

Painter

Indifferent.

Not bad.

Poet

Admirable: how this grace

It's wonderful: how well you've captured

Speaks his own standing! what a mental power
This eye shoots forth! how big imagination
Moves in this lip! to the dumbness of the gesture
One might interpret.

Painter
It is a pretty mocking of the life.
Here is a touch; is't good?

Poet
I will say of it,
It tutors nature: artificial strife
Lives in these touches, livelier than life.

Enter certain Senators, and pass over

Painter
How this lord is follow'd!

Poet
The senators of Athens: happy men!

Painter
Look, more!

Poet
You see this confluence, this great flood
of visitors.
I have, in this rough work, shaped out a man,
Whom this beneath world doth embrace and hug
With amplest entertainment: my free drift
Halts not particularly, but moves itself
In a wide sea of wax: no levell'd malice
Infects one comma in the course I hold;
But flies an eagle flight, bold and forth on,
Leaving no tract behind.

Painter
How shall I understand you?

Poet
I will unbolt to you.
You see how all conditions, how all minds,
As well of glib and slippery creatures as

---

*His position! How well you can see his
thoughts In his eyes! How well his imagination
can be seen
In his lips! One could almost interpret what
His gestures mean.*

*It's a nice copy of life.
Here's the question; is it good?*

*I would say
It teaches nature: artificial action
Comes alive in the brushstrokes, it's more
lively than life itself.*

How many followers this lord has!

The senators of Athens: lucky men!

Look, more!

*You see this merging of these great floods
of visitors.
I have, in this rough work, described a man,
Whom this mortal world embraces and hugs
With the warmest welcome: my free ideas
Don't stop for particulars, but flow across
My wax tablet: there's not a
Jot of malice in anything I write;
It flies like an eagle, boldly going forward,
Leaving no trace behind.*

What do you mean?

*I'll explain.
You see how all classes, all minds,
Shallow and dubious characters as well*

Of grave and austere quality, tender down
Their services to Lord Timon: his large fortune
Upon his good and gracious nature hanging
Subdues and properties to his love and tendance
All sorts of hearts; yea, from the glass-faced flatterer
To Apemantus, that few things loves better
Than to abhor himself: even he drops down
The knee before him, and returns in peace
Most rich in Timon's nod.

Painter
I saw them speak together.

Poet
Sir, I have upon a high and pleasant hill
Feign'd Fortune to be throned: the base o' the mount
Is rank'd with all deserts, all kind of natures,
That labour on the bosom of this sphere
To propagate their states: amongst them all,
Whose eyes are on this sovereign lady fix'd,
One do I personate of Lord Timon's frame,
Whom Fortune with her ivory hand wafts to her;
Whose present grace to present slaves and servants
Translates his rivals.

Painter
'Tis conceived to scope.
This throne, this Fortune, and this hill, methinks,
With one man beckon'd from the rest below,
Bowing his head against the steepy mount
To climb his happiness, would be well express'd
In our condition.

Poet
Nay, sir, but hear me on.
All those which were his fellows but of late,
Some better than his value, on the moment
Follow his strides, his lobbies fill with tendance,
Rain sacrificial whisperings in his ear,

As those of serious and fine quality, offer
Their services to Lord Timon: his great wealth
Combined with his good and kind nature
Draws the love and attendance of all sorts
Of people to him; from the vain flatterer
To Apemantus, who has no love for mankind,
Not even himself-even he kneels before him,
And goes home happy to have been acknowledged by Timon.

I saw them talking to each other.

Sir, I have imagined Fortune as having her throne
On top of a high and pleasant hill: the bottom of the hill
Is surrounded by all types of men, all kinds of natures,
That work on the face of the earth
To get more possessions: amongst them all,
With eyes fixed on this royal lady,
I represent one like Lord Timon,
Whom Fortune beckons with her white hand;
One whose obvious generosity makes all his rivals Look like servants and slaves.

You've hit the mark there.
This throne, this Fortune, and this hill, I think,
With one man being chosen from below,
Leaning into the steep slope to climb up
To achieve happiness, is very like our Position as artists.

No sir, listen further.
All of those who were recently his equals,
Some of them richer than him, follow after him at once, they fill up his waiting rooms,
whisper to him as if praying to gods,
even worship his stirrup as they hold it,

Make sacred even his stirrup, and through him
Drink the free air.

Painter
Ay, marry, what of these?

Poet
When Fortune in her shift and change of mood
Spurns down her late beloved, all his
dependants
Which labour'd after him to the mountain's top
Even on their knees and hands, let him slip
down,
Not one accompanying his declining foot.

Painter
'Tis common:
A thousand moral paintings I can show
That shall demonstrate these quick blows of
Fortune's
More pregnantly than words. Yet you do well
To show Lord Timon that mean eyes have seen
The foot above the head.

Trumpets sound. Enter TIMON, addressing himself courteously to every suitor; a Messenger from VENTIDIUS talking with him; LUCILIUS and other servants following

TIMON
Imprison'd is he, say you?

Messenger
Ay, my good lord: five talents is his debt,
His means most short, his creditors most strait:
Your honourable letter he desires
To those have shut him up; which failing,
Periods his comfort.

TIMON
Noble Ventidius! Well;
I am not of that feather to shake off
My friend when he must need me. I do know
him
A gentleman that well deserves a help:
Which he shall have: I'll pay the debt,
and free him.

behaving as if he gave them the air they breathe.

Yes, certainly, so what about them?

When Fortune changes her mood and pushes away the one she recently favoured, all his hangers-on, who struggled after him on his ascent, even crawling after him, let him slip down, nobody follows him as he falls.

This is commonplace; I can show you a thousand instructional paintings, that can show the quick changes of Fortune better than words. But you're doing a good thing in showing Lord Timon that even lowly eyes have seen that there are feet above one ready to stamp one down.

You say he's in prison?

Yes, my good lord; he owes five talents, he's short of money, and his creditors are very stern: he wants you to write to those who have locked him up; without that he hasn't a hope.

Noble Ventidus! Very well; I'm not the type to ignore a friend in need. I know he is a gentleman that deserves a helping hand; he shall have it. I'll pay the debt, and free him.

Messenger
Your lordship ever binds him.

He will be your servant forever.

TIMON
Commend me to him: I will send his ransom;
And being enfranchised, bid him come to me.
'Tis not enough to help the feeble up,
But to support him after. Fare you well.

*Give him my greetings: I will send the price;
once he's free, tell him to come to me.
It's not enough to help the weak man up,
one must support him afterwards. Farewell.*

Messenger
All happiness to your honour!

All happiness to your honour!

Exit

Enter an old Athenian

Old Athenian
Lord Timon, hear me speak.

Lord Timon, listen to me.

TIMON
Freely, good father.

Gladly, good old fellow.

Old Athenian
Thou hast a servant named Lucilius.

You have a servant called Lucilius.

TIMON
I have so: what of him?

I have: what about him?

Old Athenian
Most noble Timon, call the man before thee.

Most noble Timon, call him to you.

TIMON
Attends he here, or no? Lucilius!

Is he here, or not? Lucilius!

LUCILIUS
Here, at your lordship's service.

Here, at your lordship's service.

Old Athenian
This fellow here, Lord Timon, this thy creature,
By night frequents my house. I am a man
That from my first have been inclined to thrift;
And my estate deserves an heir more raised
Than one which holds a trencher.

*This fellow here, Lord Timon, this pet of yours,
hangs around my house at night. I am a man
who has always been careful to save money;
and I want an heir for my estate of a better class
than a serving man.*

TIMON
Well; what further?

I see. What else?

Old Athenian
One only daughter have I, no kin else,
On whom I may confer what I have got:
The maid is fair, o' the youngest for a bride,
And I have bred her at my dearest cost
In qualities of the best. This man of thine
Attempts her love: I prithee, noble lord,
Join with me to forbid him her resort;
Myself have spoke in vain.

*I have just one daughter, no other family,
to leave what I have to:
the girl is beautiful, just of marriageable age,
and I have brought her up at great expense
to have the best accomplishments. This man of
yours is trying to get her: I ask you, noble lord,
to join with me in forbidding him from seeing
her; I've told him myself in vain.*

TIMON
The man is honest.

The man is honest.

Old Athenian
Therefore he will be, Timon:
His honesty rewards him in itself;
It must not bear my daughter.

*So he should be, Timon:
his honesty should be its own reward;
he shan't have my daughter in addition.*

TIMON
Does she love him?

Does she love him?

Old Athenian
She is young and apt:
Our own precedent passions do instruct us
What levity's in youth.

*She is young and suggestible:
we know from our own youth
how changeable the young are.*

TIMON
[To LUCILIUS] Love you the maid?

Do you love the girl?

LUCILIUS
Ay, my good lord, and she accepts of it.

Yes, my good lord, and she returns it.

Old Athenian
If in her marriage my consent be missing,
I call the gods to witness, I will choose
Mine heir from forth the beggars of the world,
And dispossess her all.

*If she marries without my consent,
I call on the gods to witness that I shall choose
my heir from amongst the beggars of the world,
and she won't get a penny.*

TIMON
How shall she be endow'd,
if she be mated with an equal husband?

*What dowry would she get,
if she had a husband of the same class?*

Old Athenian
Three talents on the present; in future, all.

*Three talents at the moment; in future she'll
have everything.*

TIMON

This gentleman of mine hath served me long:
To build his fortune I will strain a little,
For 'tis a bond in men. Give him thy daughter:
What you bestow, in him I'll counterpoise,
And make him weigh with her.

*This gentleman of mine has served me for a
long time: I shall try and help him out a bit,
I'm obliged to. Let him marry your daughter:
what you give with her, I'll match with him,
to make them both equal.*

Old Athenian
Most noble lord,
Pawn me to this your honour, she is his.

*Most noble Lord,
if you do me this honour, he can have her.*

TIMON
My hand to thee; mine honour on my promise.

*We'll shake on it; and I give you my word I'll do
it.*

LUCILIUS
Humbly I thank your lordship: never may
The state or fortune fall into my keeping,
Which is not owed to you!

*I give your lordship my humble thanks:
for the rest of my life I'll owe
everything to you!*

Exeunt LUCILIUS and Old Athenian

Poet
Vouchsafe my labour, and long live your
lordship!

Accept my work, and long live your lordship!

TIMON
I thank you; you shall hear from me anon:
Go not away. What have you there, my friend?

*I thank you; you shall hear from me soon:
don't go away. What have you got there, my
friend?*

Painter
A piece of painting, which I do beseech
Your lordship to accept.

*A painting, which I beg
your lordship to accept.*

TIMON
Painting is welcome.
The painting is almost the natural man;
or since dishonour traffics with man's nature,
He is but outside: these pencill'd figures are
Even such as they give out. I like your work;
And you shall find I like it: wait attendance
Till you hear further from me.

*I like paintings.
Paintings are almost like man as he really is;
when dishonest reports make a man better than
he is,
you can't see him: these painted figures are
exactly what they seem. I like your work;
and you shall see that I like it: stick around
until you hear from me again.*

Painter
The gods preserve ye!

May the gods preserve you!

TIMON
Well fare you, gentleman: give me your hand;

Farewell, gentlemen: give me your hand;

We must needs dine together. Sir, your jewel
Hath suffer'd under praise.

Jeweller
What, my lord! dispraise?

TIMON
A more satiety of commendations.
If I should pay you for't as 'tis extoll'd,
It would unclew me quite.

Jeweller
My lord, 'tis rated
As those which sell would give: but you well know,
Things of like value differing in the owners
Are prized by their masters: believe't, dear lord,
You mend the jewel by the wearing it.

TIMON
Well mock'd.

Merchant
No, my good lord; he speaks the common tongue,
Which all men speak with him.

TIMON
Look, who comes here: will you be chid?

Enter APEMANTUS

Jeweller
We'll bear, with your lordship.

Merchant
He'll spare none.

TIMON
Good morrow to thee, gentle Apemantus!

APEMANTUS
Till I be gentle, stay thou for thy good morrow;
When thou art Timon's dog, and these knaves honest.

---

we must dine together. Sir, your jewel seems less likely to sell, due to the praise it's had.

What, my lord! Have people been criticising it?

No, it's been loaded with praise. If I paid you according to the amount of praise, it would ruin me.

My Lord, it's valued by what the sellers would pay for it: but you well know that things are given different values depending upon who owns them: believe me, dear lord, you increase its value by wearing it.

Nicely played.

No, my good lord; he's only saying what everyone else says.

Look who's coming: do you want to be told off?

We can stand it if your lordship can.

He won't spare anyone.

Good day to you, gentle Apemantus!

You won't get a greeting from me until I am polite; when you have turned into your dog, and these knaves have turned honest.

TIMON
Why dost thou call them knaves? thou know'st
them not.

*What you call them knaves? You don't know
them.*

APEMANTUS
Are they not Athenians?

They are Athenians, aren't they?

TIMON
Yes.

Yes.

APEMANTUS
Then I repent not.

Then I stick to what I said.

Jeweller
You know me, Apemantus?

Do you know me, Apemantus?

APEMANTUS
Thou know'st I do: I call'd thee by thy name.

You know I do: I called you by your name.

TIMON
Thou art proud, Apemantus.

You are proud, Apemantus.

APEMANTUS
Of nothing so much as that I am not like
Timon.

Mainly of the fact that I am not like Timon.

TIMON
Whither art going?

Where are you going?

APEMANTUS
To knock out an honest Athenian's brains.

To knock out the brains of an honest Athenian.

TIMON
That's a deed thou'lt die for.

You'll be hanged for that.

APEMANTUS
Right, if doing nothing be death by the law.

Yes, if doing nothing is a capital offence.

TIMON
How likest thou this picture, Apemantus?

What do you think of this picture, Apemantus?

APEMANTUS
The best, for the innocence.

I like its simplicity best.

TIMON
Wrought he not well that painted it?

Didn't the painter do it well?

APEMANTUS
He wrought better that made the painter; and yet
he's but a filthy piece of work.

The one who made the painter did better; but he's still a filthy piece of work.

Painter
You're a dog.

You're a dog.

APEMANTUS
Thy mother's of my generation: what's she, if I be a dog?

*Your mother is the same as me: what's she, if I'm a
dog?*

TIMON
Wilt dine with me, Apemantus?

Will you dine with me, Apemantus?

APEMANTUS
No; I eat not lords.

No; I don't eat lords.

TIMON
An thou shouldst, thou 'ldst anger ladies.

If you did, you would upset ladies.

APEMANTUS
O, they eat lords; so they come by great bellies.

Oh, they eat lords; that's how they get swollen bellies.

TIMON
That's a lascivious apprehension.

That's a dirty thought.

APEMANTUS
So thou apprehendest it: take it for thy labour.

That's how you look at it; you're welcome to it.

TIMON
How dost thou like this jewel, Apemantus?

What do you think of this jewel, Apemantus?

APEMANTUS
Not so well as plain-dealing, which will not cost a
man a doit.

*I don't like it as much as honest dealing, which doesn't cost
a man a cent.*

TIMON
What dost thou think 'tis worth?

What do you think it's worth?

APEMANTUS
Not worth my thinking. How now, poet!

It's not worth my thinking about. Hello there, poet!

Poet
How now, philosopher!

Hello there, philosopher!

APEMANTUS
Thou liest.

You're lying.

Poet
Art not one?

Aren't you one?

APEMANTUS
Yes.

Yes.

Poet
Then I lie not.

Then I'm not lying.

APEMANTUS
Art not a poet?

Aren't you a poet?

Poet
Yes.

Yes.

APEMANTUS
Then thou liest: look in thy last work, where thou
hast feigned him a worthy fellow.

*Then you are lying: look in your last work, where you
described Timon as a good fellow.*

Poet
That's not feigned; he is so.

That's not lying; he is.

APEMANTUS
Yes, he is worthy of thee, and to pay thee for thy
labour: he that loves to be flattered is worthy o'
the flatterer. Heavens, that I were a lord!

*Yes, he's good for you, to pay you for your
work: someone loves to be flattered deserves
to have to put up with flatterers. Gods, I wish I
were a lord!*

TIMON
What wouldst do then, Apemantus?

What would you do then, Apemantus?

APEMANTUS
E'en as Apemantus does now; hate a lord with
my heart.

*Just the same as I do now; I would hate a lord
with all my heart.*

TIMON
What, thyself?

What, yourself?

APEMANTUS
Ay.

Yes.

TIMON

Wherefore?

Why?

APEMANTUS
That I had no angry wit to be a lord.
Art not thou a merchant?

That I was so stupid as to want to be a lord.
Aren't you a merchant?

Merchant
Ay, Apemantus.

Yes, Apemantus.

APEMANTUS
Traffic confound thee, if the gods will not!

May trade defeat you, if the gods will not!

Merchant
If traffic do it, the gods do it.

If trade did it, that means the gods did it.

APEMANTUS
Traffic's thy god; and thy god confound thee!

Trade is your god; and may your god defeat
you!

Trumpet sounds. Enter a Messenger

TIMON
What trumpet's that?

What's that trumpet?

Messenger
'Tis Alcibiades, and some twenty horse,
All of companionship.

It's Alcibiades, with about twenty cavalry,
all equals.

TIMON
Pray, entertain them; give them guide to us.

Please, welcome them; guide them here.

Exeunt some Attendants

You must needs dine with me: go not you
hence
Till I have thank'd you: when dinner's done,
Show me this piece. I am joyful of your sights.

You must dine with me: don't go
until I thank you: when dinner's over,
show me this piece. I am glad to see you.

Enter ALCIBIADES, with the rest

Most welcome, sir!

You're very welcome, sir!

APEMANTUS
So, so, there!
Aches contract and starve your supple joints!
That there should be small love 'mongst these
sweet knaves,

Well, well!
May pain invade and destroy your supple
joints!
To think there is so little love lost between these

And all this courtesy! The strain of man's bred out
Into baboon and monkey.

cunning knaves, and there's so much politeness! Men are evolving into baboons and monkeys.

ALCIBIADES
Sir, you have saved my longing, and I feed
Most hungerly on your sight.

*Sir, you are just what I want to see,
I'm gorging myself on the sight.*

TIMON
Right welcome, sir!
Ere we depart, we'll share a bounteous time
In different pleasures. Pray you, let us in.

*You're very welcome, sir!
Before we part, we will have an excellent time
at various diversions. If you please, let's go in.*

Exeunt all except APEMANTUS

Enter two Lords

First Lord
What time o' day is't, Apemantus?

What time is it, Apemantus?

APEMANTUS
Time to be honest.

It's time to be honest.

First Lord
That time serves still.

It's always time for that.

APEMANTUS
The more accursed thou, that still omitt'st it.

Then you are all the worse, for failing to be so.

Second Lord
Thou art going to Lord Timon's feast?

Are you going to Lord Timon's feast?

APEMANTUS
Ay, to see meat fill knaves and wine heat fools.

Yes, to see knaves filled with meat and fools heated by wine.

Second Lord
Fare thee well, fare thee well.

Farewell, farewell.

APEMANTUS
Thou art a fool to bid me farewell twice.

You're a fool to say farewell twice.

Second Lord
Why, Apemantus?

Why, Apemantus?

APEMANTUS
Shouldst have kept one to thyself, for I mean to

You should have kept one for yourself, for I

20

give thee none.

don't intend to give you one.

First Lord
Hang thyself!

Go and hang yourself!

APEMANTUS
No, I will do nothing at thy bidding: make thy requests to thy friend.

No, I'll do nothing you tell me to: ask your friend.

Second Lord
Away, unpeaceable dog, or I'll spurn thee hence!

Go away, you quarrelsome dog, or I'll kick you out of here.

APEMANTUS
I will fly, like a dog, the heels o' the ass.

Like a dog, I'll flee from the heels of an ass.

Exit

First Lord
He's opposite to humanity. Come, shall we in,
And taste Lord Timon's bounty? he outgoes
The very heart of kindness.

He is against all mankind. Come, shall we go in, and sample Lord Timon's hospitality? He's more generous than generosity itself.

Second Lord
He pours it out; Plutus, the god of gold,
Is but his steward: no meed, but he repays
Sevenfold above itself; no gift to him,
But breeds the giver a return exceeding
All use of quittance.

He has a very free hand; Plutus, the god of gold, is only his servant. Every good thing gets a reward
seven times what it deserves; there is no gift that isn't repaid with interest.

First Lord
The noblest mind he carries
That ever govern'd man.

He has the noblest mind any man ever had.

Second Lord
Long may he live in fortunes! Shall we in?

May he remain prosperous forever! Shall we go in?

First Lord
I'll keep you company.

I'll come with you.

Exeunt

SCENE II. A banqueting-room in Timon's house.

Hautboys playing loud music. A great banquet served in; FLAVIUS and others attending; then enter TIMON, ALCIBIADES, Lords, Senators, and VENTIDIUS. Then comes, dropping, after all, APEMANTUS, discontentedly, like himself

VENTIDIUS
Most honour'd Timon,
It hath pleased the gods to remember my father's age,
And call him to long peace.
He is gone happy, and has left me rich:
Then, as in grateful virtue I am bound
To your free heart, I do return those talents,
Doubled with thanks and service, from whose help
I derived liberty.

*Most honoured Timon,
the gods have been pleased to recall my father's age,
and call him to his long rest.
He has died happy, and has left me rich:
so, as I owe such a debt of gratitude
to your generosity, I return these talents,
which bought my freedom, with my
thanks and respect.*

TIMON
O, by no means,
Honest Ventidius; you mistake my love:
I gave it freely ever; and there's none
Can truly say he gives, if he receives:
If our betters play at that game, we must not dare
To imitate them; faults that are rich are fair.

*Oh, I won't take them,
honest Ventidius; you don't understand my love:
I always give it freely; and nobody
can really call himself a giver, if he receives:
if our betters play that game, we shouldn't dare
imitate them; the rich can get away with more.*

VENTIDIUS
A noble spirit!

A noble spirit!

TIMON
Nay, my lords,

No, my lords,

[They all stand ceremoniously looking on]

Ceremony was but devised at first
To set a gloss on faint deeds, hollow welcomes,
Recanting goodness, sorry ere 'tis shown;
But where there is true friendship, there needs none.
Pray, sit; more welcome are ye to my fortunes
Than my fortunes to me.

*ceremonies were only invented
to improve the look of trivial deeds, hollow welcomes, false goodness, which is regretted before it's shown; when there's true friendship you don't need ceremony. Please, sit; you are more welcome to my fortune than my fortune is to me.*

They sit

First Lord

My lord, we always have confess'd it.

APEMANTUS
Ho, ho, confess'd it! hang'd it, have you not?

TIMON
O, Apemantus, you are welcome.

APEMANTUS
No;
You shall not make me welcome:
I come to have thee thrust me out of doors.

TIMON
Fie, thou'rt a churl; ye've got a humour there
Does not become a man: 'tis much to blame.
They say, my lords, 'ira furor brevis est;' but yond
man is ever angry. Go, let him have a table by
himself, for he does neither affect company, nor is
he fit for't, indeed.

APEMANTUS
Let me stay at thine apperil, Timon: I come to
observe; I give thee warning on't.

TIMON
I take no heed of thee; thou'rt an Athenian,
therefore welcome: I myself would have no power;
prithee, let my meat make thee silent.

APEMANTUS
I scorn thy meat; 'twould choke me, for I should
ne'er flatter thee. O you gods, what a number of
men eat Timon, and he sees 'em not! It grieves me
to see so many dip their meat in one man's blood;
and all the madness is, he cheers them up too.
I wonder men dare trust themselves with men:
Methinks they should invite them without knives;
Good for their meat, and safer for their lives.
There's much example for't; the fellow that sits

My lord, we have always admitted it.

Ho ho, admitted it! You've hanged it, haven't you?

Oh, Apemantus, you are welcome.

No;
you will not make me welcome:
I have come for you to kick me out.

Blast you, you're a miserable devil; you've got a temper there
which doesn't suit a man: it's very bad.
They say, my lords, that anger is a brief madness; but that
man is always angry. Give him a table to himself, for he doesn't like company, and in fact he's not fit for it.

You let me stay at your own risk, Timon: I've come to watch, I warn you.

I take no notice of you; you're an Athenian, so you are welcome: I can't keep you quiet, but perhaps my meat can.

I reject your meat; it would choke me, being for flatterers,
and I will never flatter you. Oh you gods, how many
men eat Timon, and he can't see it! It makes me sad
to see so many dipping their meat in the blood of one man;
and the mad thing is, he encourages them.
It amazes me that men dare to trust other men:
I think they should invite them without their knives;

next him now, parts bread with him, pledges the
breath of him in a divided draught, is the readiest
man to kill him: 't has been proved. If I were a
huge man, I should fear to drink at meals;
Lest they should spy my windpipe's dangerous notes:
Great men should drink with harness on their throats.

TIMON
My lord, in heart; and let the health go round.

Second Lord
Let it flow this way, my good lord.

APEMANTUS
Flow this way! A brave fellow! he keeps his tides
well. Those healths will make thee and thy state
look ill, Timon. Here's that which is too weak to
be a sinner, honest water, which ne'er left man i' the mire:
This and my food are equals; there's no odds:
Feasts are too proud to give thanks to the gods.
Apemantus' grace.
Immortal gods, I crave no pelf;
I pray for no man but myself:
Grant I may never prove so fond,
To trust man on his oath or bond;
Or a harlot, for her weeping;
Or a dog, that seems a-sleeping:
Or a keeper with my freedom;
Or my friends, if I should need 'em.
Amen. So fall to't:
Rich men sin, and I eat root.
Eats and drinks
Much good dich thy good heart, Apemantus!

TIMON
Captain Alcibiades, your heart's in the field now.

ALCIBIADES

they would save their meat, and it would be safer for their lives.
There are many instances of it; the man that sits next to him now, shares the bread with him, drinks his health from a shared cup, is the one who is readiest to kill him: everyone knows this.
If I were a great man, I would be afraid to drink at meals, in case they saw the vulnerable places on my neck: great men should drink with armour round their throats.

My lord, your good health; and let the toast go round.

Let it flow this way, my good lord.

Flow this way! A bold chap! He keeps his eye on the tide.
All this drinking of healths will actually make you ill, Timon.
Here's something which is too weak to cause sin,
honest water, which never left any man in trouble:
my food is much the same, there is no difference between them:
those who eat feasts are too proud to give thanks to the gods.
Immortal gods, I want no money;
I'm praying for no one but myself.
Never let me become so stupid,
as to trust a man on his oath or word;
or believe a harlot's tears,
or a dog that seems to be asleep,
or a jailer with my freedom,
all my friends, when I need them. Amen.
And so let's eat:
rich men sin, and I eat vegetables.

Captain Alcibiades, your heart is on the battlefield.

My heart is ever at your service, my lord.

TIMON
You had rather be at a breakfast of enemies than a
dinner of friends.

ALCIBIADES
So they were bleeding-new, my lord, there's no meat
like 'em: I could wish my best friend at such a feast.

APEMANTUS
Would all those flatterers were thine enemies then,
that then thou mightst kill 'em and bid me to 'em!

First Lord
Might we but have that happiness, my lord, that you
would once use our hearts, whereby we might express
some part of our zeals, we should think ourselves
for ever perfect.

TIMON
O, no doubt, my good friends, but the gods themselves have provided that I shall have much help
from you: how had you been my friends else? why
have you that charitable title from thousands, did
not you chiefly belong to my heart? I have told
more of you to myself than you can with modesty
speak in your own behalf; and thus far I confirm
you. O you gods, think I, what need we have any
friends, if we should ne'er have need of 'em? they
were the most needless creatures living, should

My heart is always at your service, my lord.

*You'd rather be having breakfast with your enemies than
dinner with your friends.*

*Provided they were newly bleeding, my lord, there's no meat
to match them: I'd wish my best friend was at such a feast.*

*I wish all these flatterers were your enemies then,
then you might kill them and ask me to eat them!*

*I wish we could have the privilege, my lord, of you just once putting our affection to the test, so that
we could show a little part of our enthusiasm, that would
make us happy for ever.*

*Oh, do not doubt, my good friends, that the gods
have made sure I get great comfort from you: otherwise why would you be my friend? Why
do you have that loving title from the thousands I could choose from,
if you're not firmly in my heart. I have commended
you more to myself than you could with modesty say
on your own behalf; and so I confirm your position as my friends. Oh you
gods, I think, what need do we have of any friends, if we
never have any need of them? They would be the most*

25

we
ne'er have use for 'em, and would most resemble
sweet instruments hung up in cases that keep their
sounds to themselves. Why, I have often wished
myself poorer, that I might come nearer to you. We
are born to do benefits: and what better or
properer can we can our own than the riches of our
friends? O, what a precious comfort 'tis, to have
so many, like brothers, commanding one another's
fortunes! O joy, e'en made away ere 't can be born!
Mine eyes cannot hold out water, methinks: to
forget their faults, I drink to you.

APEMANTUS
Thou weepest to make them drink, Timon.

Second Lord
Joy had the like conception in our eyes
And at that instant like a babe sprung up.

APEMANTUS
Ho, ho! I laugh to think that babe a bastard.

Third Lord
I promise you, my lord, you moved me much.

APEMANTUS
Much!

Tucket, within

TIMON
What means that trump?

Enter a Servant
How now?

Servant
Please you, my lord, there are certain

*useless creatures living if we never had a use for
them, they would be like sweet instruments
hung up in cases, that keep their sounds to
themselves.
Why, I have often wished that I was poorer so I
might be closer to you. We are born to do good;
what is it more right that we can call our own
than the riches of our friends? Oh what a great
comfort it is to have so many sharing each
other's
fortunes like brothers. It's a joy that appears
(because of tears)
to disappear before it even starts! I don't think I
can keep
from weeping. To cover up my faults, I drink
your health.*

Your crying makes them drink, Timon.

*We have the same joy as you,
it's mirrored in our eyes.*

*Ho, Ho! It makes me laugh to think how
insincere you are.*

*I promise you, my lord, I found that very
moving.*

Very!

What does that trumpet mean?

What's going on?

If you please, my lord, there are certain

26

ladies most desirous of admittance.

ladies who are very keen to see you.

TIMON
Ladies! what are their wills?

Ladies! What do they want?

Servant
There comes with them a forerunner, my lord, which
bears that office, to signify their pleasures.

They have a Herald with them, my lord, who has that position to tell you what they want.

TIMON
I pray, let them be admitted.

Please, let them in.

Enter Cupid

Cupid
Hail to thee, worthy Timon, and to all
That of his bounties taste! The five best senses
Acknowledge thee their patron; and come freely
To gratulate thy plenteous bosom: th' ear,
Taste, touch and smell, pleased from thy table rise;
They only now come but to feast thine eyes.

*Greetings to you, good Timon, and to everyone sharing his generosity! The five great senses acknowledge you as their master; they have come
to praise your generosity: hearing, taste, touch and smell, have been satisfied at your table;
all you need now is a feast for your eyes.*

TIMON
They're welcome all; let 'em have kind admittance:
Music, make their welcome!

They are all welcome; let them come in; play the music to welcome them!

Exit Cupid

First Lord
You see, my lord, how ample you're beloved.

You see, my lord, how much you're loved.

Music. Re-enter Cupid with a mask of Ladies as Amazons, with lutes in their hands, dancing and playing

APEMANTUS
Hoy-day, what a sweep of vanity comes this way!
They dance! they are mad women.
Like madness is the glory of this life.
As this pomp shows to a little oil and root.
We make ourselves fools, to disport ourselves;
And spend our flatteries, to drink those men

*Hello!
What a parade of frivolity is coming.
All dancing! They are mad women.
Vanity is a madness of this life, so is having all this food when all you need is a little oil and vegetables.
We make fools of ourselves to keep ourselves*

Upon whose age we void it up again,
With poisonous spite and envy.
Who lives that's not depraved or depraves?
Who dies, that bears not one spurn to their graves
Of their friends' gift?
I should fear those that dance before me now
Would one day stamp upon me: 't has been done;
Men shut their doors against a setting sun.

occupied, we flatter to win over men whom in old age we reject again, full of poisonous spite and envy. Who is there alive who's not either slandered or a slanderer? Who dies who doesn't carry a single insult to their grave given to them by a friend? I would be afraid that those dancing in front of me now would one day stamp on me. It happens. Men aren't interested in you when you fall.

The Lords rise from table, with much adoring of TIMON; and to show their loves, each singles out an Amazon, and all dance, men with women, a lofty strain or two to the hautboys, and cease

TIMON
You have done our pleasures much grace, fair ladies,
Set a fair fashion on our entertainment,
Which was not half so beautiful and kind;
You have added worth unto 't and lustre,
And entertain'd me with mine own device;
I am to thank you for 't.

You've lent much grace to our enjoyment, fair ladies, given our entertainment such an attractive appearance, it wasn't half so beautiful and gracious before; you have added goodness and glamour, and use my own entertainment to entertain me; I want to thank you for it.

First Lady
My lord, you take us even at the best.

My lord, you give us our best praise.

APEMANTUS
'Faith, for the worst is filthy; and would not hold
taking, I doubt me.

I swear, you wouldn't want to be given the worst, it's filthy.

TIMON
Ladies, there is an idle banquet attends you:
Please you to dispose yourselves.

Ladies, there's a little banquet waiting for you: please help yourselves.

All Ladies
Most thankfully, my lord.

Very gratefully, my lord.

Exeunt Cupid and Ladies

TIMON
Flavius.

Flavius.

FLAVIUS
My lord?

My lord?

TIMON
The little casket bring me hither.

Bring the little casket here to me.

FLAVIUS
Yes, my lord. [Aside] More jewels yet!
There is no crossing him in 's humour;
Else I should tell him well, i' faith I should,
When all's spent, he 'ld be cross'd then, an he could.
'Tis pity bounty had not eyes behind,
That man might ne'er be wretched for his mind.

Yes, my lord. [aside] Still more jewels!
There's no stopping his madness;
otherwise I would tell him firmly, I really
would, that when it's all gone he'll be in debt.
Generosity should have eyes in the back of his
head,
so a man could never be ruined by being kind.

Exit

First Lord
Where be our men?

Where are our men?

Servant
Here, my lord, in readiness.

Here, my lord, all ready.

Second Lord
Our horses!

Our horses!

Re-enter FLAVIUS, with the casket

TIMON
O my friends,
I have one word to say to you: look you, my good lord,
I must entreat you, honour me so much
As to advance this jewel; accept it and wear it,
Kind my lord.

O my friends,
I just want a word with you: see here, my good
lord,
I must beg you, do me the honour
of polishing this jewel by accepting it and
wearing it, my kind lord.

First Lord
I am so far already in your gifts,--

I'm already so indebted to you–

All
So are we all.

So are all of us.

Enter a Servant

Servant
My lord, there are certain nobles of the senate
Newly alighted, and come to visit you.

My lord, there are certain noblemen from the
Senate who have just landed and have come to
visit you.

TIMON

They are fairly welcome.

They are most welcome.

FLAVIUS
I beseech your honour,
Vouchsafe me a word; it does concern you
near.

I beg your honour,
let me have a word; it concerns you intimately.

TIMON
Near! why then, another time I'll hear thee:
I prithee, let's be provided to show them
entertainment.

Concerns me! Well then, it can wait to another
time: please, let's get on and give them a good
welcome.

FLAVIUS
[Aside] I scarce know how.

I don't know what to do.

Enter a Second Servant

Second Servant
May it please your honour, Lord Lucius,
Out of his free love, hath presented to you
Four milk-white horses, trapp'd in silver.

If you please, your honour, Lord Lucius,
from his love for you, has presented you with
four milk white horses, with silver harnesses.

TIMON
I shall accept them fairly; let the presents
Be worthily entertain'd.

I shall accept them politely; let the presents
be given the attention they deserve.

Enter a third Servant

How now! what news?

Third Servant
Please you, my lord, that honourable
gentleman, Lord Lucullus, entreats your
company
to-morrow to hunt with him, and has sent your
honour
two brace of greyhounds.

If you please, my lord, that honourable
gentlemen, Lord Lucullus, asks you to go
hunting
with him tomorrow, and he has sent your
honour
two pairs of greyhounds.

TIMON
I'll hunt with him; and let them be received,
Not without fair reward.

I'll hunt with him; and welcome the dogs,
which will be paid for.

FLAVIUS
[Aside] What will this come to?
He commands us to provide, and give great
gifts,

What will this come to?
He tells us to lay on entertainment, and gives
great gifts,

And all out of an empty coffer:
Nor will he know his purse, or yield me this,
To show him what a beggar his heart is,
Being of no power to make his wishes good:
His promises fly so beyond his state
That what he speaks is all in debt; he owes
For every word: he is so kind that he now
Pays interest for 't; his land's put to their books.
Well, would I were gently put out of office
Before I were forced out!
Happier is he that has no friend to feed
Than such that do e'en enemies exceed.
I bleed inwardly for my lord.

and all the time there is no money in the bank:
he doesn't want to know his balance, and won't
allow me to show him that his heart has become
a beggar, which has no power to make up the
shortfall: what he promises is so far beyond
what he has that everything he says puts him in
debt; he owes for every word: he is so kind that
he is now paying interest for it; his land is all
mortgaged. Well, I would rather quietly leave
the job before being forced out!
You're better off having no friends to feed
than having ones that make more demands on
you then enemies do.
I suffer in silence for my lord.

Exit

TIMON
You do yourselves
Much wrong, you bate too much of your own
merits:
Here, my lord, a trifle of our love.

You do yourselves
an injustice, you put your own merits down too
much:
here, my lord, a little sign of our friendship.

Second Lord
With more than common thanks I will receive
it.

I will take it with great thanks.

Third Lord
O, he's the very soul of bounty!

Oh, he's the very soul of generosity!

TIMON
And now I remember, my lord, you gave
Good words the other day of a bay courser
I rode on: it is yours, because you liked it.

And now I remember, my lord, you said
kind words the other day about a bay hunter
I was riding: it's yours, because you liked it.

Second Lord
O, I beseech you, pardon me, my lord, in that.

Oh, I beg you, you mustn't give me that, my
lord.

TIMON
You may take my word, my lord; I know, no
man
Can justly praise but what he does affect:
I weigh my friend's affection with mine own;
I'll tell you true. I'll call to you.

You can take me at my word, my lord, I know
men only truly praise what they desire:
my friends' desires are just as important as my
own,
I assure you. I'll call on you.

All Lords
O, none so welcome.

Oh, nobody would be more welcome.

TIMON
I take all and your several visitations
So kind to heart, 'tis not enough to give;
Methinks, I could deal kingdoms to my friends,
And ne'er be weary. Alcibiades,
Thou art a soldier, therefore seldom rich;
It comes in charity to thee: for all thy living
Is 'mongst the dead, and all the lands thou hast
Lie in a pitch'd field.

I take so much pleasure from all your visits, I don't have enough to give; I think I could give out kingdoms to my friends, and never get tired of it. Alcibiades, you are a soldier, and so rarely rich; whatever you receive is true charity: because all your work is among the dead, and all your estates lie on the battlefield.

ALCIBIADES
Ay, defiled land, my lord.

Yes, defiled land, my lord.

First Lord
We are so virtuously bound--

We are so wonderfully obliged—

TIMON
And so
Am I to you.

And so am I to you.

Second Lord
So infinitely endear'd--

So hugely indebted—

TIMON
All to you. Lights, more lights!

That's all on my side. Lights, more lights!

First Lord
The best of happiness,
Honour and fortunes, keep with you, Lord
Timon!

Made the greatest happiness, honour and fortune, remain with you, Lord Timon!

TIMON
Ready for his friends.

So I can serve my friends.

Exeunt all but APEMANTUS and TIMON

APEMANTUS
What a coil's here!
Serving of becks and jutting-out of bums!
I doubt whether their legs be worth the sums
That are given for 'em. Friendship's full of dregs:
Methinks, false hearts should never have sound legs,
Thus honest fools lay out their wealth on court'sies.

What a farce this is! All this bowing and scraping! I doubt their bows are worth the amount you paid for them. Friendship is full of scum: I think false hearts should never have good legs, it makes honest fools give money to anyone who bows to them.

TIMON
Now, Apemantus, if thou wert not sullen, I would be
good to thee.

Now, Apemantus, if you weren't so sullen, I would be
generous to you.

APEMANTUS
No, I'll nothing: for if I should be bribed too,
there would be none left to rail upon thee, and then
thou wouldst sin the faster. Thou givest so long,
Timon, I fear me thou wilt give away thyself in
paper shortly: what need these feasts, pomps and
vain-glories?

No, I'll take nothing: if I should be bribed too,
there would be nobody left to criticise you, and then
you would be even worse. You've been giving for so long,
Timon, I fear all you'll have to give will be IOUs
shortly: what necessity is there for these feasts, parties and vanities?

TIMON
Nay, an you begin to rail on society once, I am
sworn not to give regard to you. Farewell; and come
with better music.

No, if you're going to start criticising friendship,
I swear I won't listen to you. Farewell; come back
with something better to say.

Exit

APEMANTUS
So:
Thou wilt not hear me now; thou shalt not then:
I'll lock thy heaven from thee.
O, that men's ears should be
To counsel deaf, but not to flattery!

So.
You won't listen to me now; you won't get a
chance later: I'll keep what could keep you
happy from you. What a state of affairs when
men are deaf to advice, but not to flattery!

Exit

Act 2

SCENE I. A Senator's house.

Enter Senator, with papers in his hand

Senator
And late, five thousand: to Varro and to Isidore
He owes nine thousand; besides my former sum,
Which makes it five and twenty. Still in motion
Of raging waste? It cannot hold; it will not.
If I want gold, steal but a beggar's dog,
And give it Timon, why, the dog coins gold.
If I would sell my horse, and buy twenty more
Better than he, why, give my horse to Timon,
Ask nothing, give it him, it foals me, straight,
And able horses. No porter at his gate,
But rather one that smiles and still invites
All that pass by. It cannot hold: no reason
Can sound his state in safety. Caphis, ho!
Caphis, I say!

Enter CAPHIS

CAPHIS
Here, sir; what is your pleasure?

Senator
Get on your cloak, and haste you to Lord Timon;
Importune him for my moneys; be not ceased
With slight denial, nor then silenced when--
'Commend me to your master'--and the cap
Plays in the right hand, thus: but tell him,
My uses cry to me, I must serve my turn
Out of mine own; his days and times are past
And my reliances on his fracted dates
Have smit my credit: I love and honour him,
But must not break my back to heal his finger;
Immediate are my needs, and my relief
Must not be toss'd and turn'd to me in words,
But find supply immediate. Get you gone:
Put on a most importunate aspect,
A visage of demand; for, I do fear,
When every feather sticks in his own wing,
Lord Timon will be left a naked gull,
Which flashes now a phoenix. Get you gone.

And recently, five thousand: to Varro and to Isidore he owes nine thousand; there's my previous amount in addition, which makes it twenty-five thousand. Still throwing it about? He can't keep this up. If I want gold, I'd just have to steal a beggar's dog and give it to Timon–why, the dog would crap money; if I wanted to sell my horse and buy twenty better ones–why, I would give my horse to Timon; I wouldn't ask him for anything, just give it to him and straightaway he would give me excellent horses. There's no guard at his gate, just someone who smiles and invites everyone who passes to come in. It can't last; there's no way of looking at it that makes it sound. Caphis, come here! Caphis, hello!

I'm here, sir; what can I do for you?

Put on your cloak, and hurry to Lord Timon; tell him I want my money; don't be put off by little excuses, or be silenced when he says 'give your master my compliments' and doffs his hat to you, like this–but tell him that I am hard pressed; I must pay my debts out of my own money; the time he should have paid has passed: and my reliance on his broken promises has damaged my credit. I love and honour him, but I can't break my back to heal his finger. I need my money at once, and I can't get any relief from polite words, I need hard cash at once. Off you go; put on a very stern face, one that won't take no for an answer: for I fear, when all the property has been claimed by its rightful owners, Lord Timon will be left like a naked gull, where now he's a Phoenix. Off you go.

CAPHIS
I go, sir.

I'm going, sir.

Senator
Ay go, sir!--Take the bonds along with you,
And have the dates in compt.

Yes, go, sir! Take the papers with you,
and have the dates of them to hand.

CAPHIS
I will, sir.

I will, sir.

Senator
Go.

Go.

Exeunt

SCENE II. The same. A hall in Timon's house.

Enter FLAVIUS, with many bills in his hand

FLAVIUS
No care, no stop! so senseless of expense,
That he will neither know how to maintain it,
Nor cease his flow of riot: takes no account
How things go from him, nor resumes no care
Of what is to continue: never mind
Was to be so unwise, to be so kind.
What shall be done? he will not hear, till feel:
I must be round with him, now he comes from
hunting.
Fie, fie, fie, fie!

*He doesn't care, and won't stop! He's so
unaware of money that he doesn't know how to
carry on nor how to stop: he doesn't pay
attention to his outgoings and gives no thought
to how he'll carry on: nobody was ever
so foolish, to be so kind.
What's to be done? He won't listen until he
feels it: I must speak to him plainly, now, as he
returns from hunting.
Damn it all!*

Enter CAPHIS, and the Servants of Isidore and Varro

CAPHIS
Good even, Varro: what,
You come for money?

*Good afternoon, Varro: what's this,
you've come for money?*

Varro's Servant
Is't not your business too?

Isn't that what you're after too?

CAPHIS
It is: and yours too, Isidore?

It is. You as well, Isisdore's man?

Isidore's Servant
It is so.

That's right.

CAPHIS
Would we were all discharged!

I wish this would all be settled!

Varro's Servant
I fear it.

I have my doubts.

CAPHIS
Here comes the lord.

Here comes the lord.

Enter TIMON, ALCIBIADES, and Lords, & c

My Alcibiades. With me? what is your will?

TIMON
So soon as dinner's done, we'll forth again,

As soon as we've had dinner, we'll go out again, friend Alcibiades. You want me? What do you want?

CAPHIS
My lord, here is a note of certain dues.

My lord, I have here a note of some debts that are due payment.

TIMON
Dues! Whence are you?

Debts! Where are you from?

CAPHIS
Of Athens here, my lord.

From here in Athens, my lord.

TIMON
Go to my steward.

Go and see my steward.

CAPHIS
Please it your lordship, he hath put me off
To the succession of new days this month:
My master is awaked by great occasion
To call upon his own, and humbly prays you
That with your other noble parts you'll suit
In giving him his right.

If you please, your lordship, he has fobbed me off from one day to the next this month: my master has very important business which means he needs his money, and he humbly requests that you'll be as noble in this as you are in everything, and pay him what you owe.

TIMON
Mine honest friend,
I prithee, but repair to me next morning.

My honest friend, I'll just ask you to come back tomorrow morning.

CAPHIS
Nay, good my lord,--

No, my good lord -

TIMON
Contain thyself, good friend.

Be calm, good friend.

Varro's Servant
One Varro's servant, my good lord,--

I am Varro's servant, my good lord -

Isidore's Servant
From Isidore;
He humbly prays your speedy payment.

I am Isidore's servant; he humbly requests that you pay him at once.

CAPHIS
If you did know, my lord, my master's wants--

If you only knew, my lord, what my master needs -

Varro's Servant
'Twas due on forfeiture, my lord, six weeks and past.

You were due to pay a forfeit, my lord, more than six weeks ago.

Isidore's Servant
Your steward puts me off, my lord;

Your steward keeps fobbing me off, my lord;

And I am sent expressly to your lordship.

TIMON
Give me breath.
I do beseech you, good my lords, keep on;
I'll wait upon you instantly.

Exeunt ALCIBIADES and Lords

To FLAVIUS
Come hither: pray you,
How goes the world, that I am thus encounter'd
With clamourous demands of date-broke bonds,
And the detention of long-since-due debts,
Against my honour?

FLAVIUS
Please you, gentlemen,
The time is unagreeable to this business:
Your importunacy cease till after dinner,
That I may make his lordship understand
Wherefore you are not paid.

TIMON
Do so, my friends. See them well entertain'd.

Exit

FLAVIUS
Pray, draw near.

Exit

Enter APEMANTUS and Fool

CAPHIS
Stay, stay, here comes the fool with
Apemantus:
let's ha' some sport with 'em.

Varro's Servant
Hang him, he'll abuse us.

Isidore's Servant
A plague upon him, dog!

and I have been sent to see your lordship in person.

Give me room to breathe.
I beg you, my good lords, go on;
I'll be with you in a moment.

Come here: I ask you,
what have things come to, for me to be attacked
with noisy demands for overdue bonds,
and accusations of unpaid debts,
calling my honour into question?

If you please, gentlemen,
this isn't a good time for this business:
postpone your demands until after dinner,
so I can help his lordship to understand
why you haven't been paid.

Do that, my friends. Make sure they are well fed.

Now, please come with me.

Wait, wait, here comes the fool with
Apemantus:
let's have some fun with them.

Hang him, he'll abuse us.

Curse him, the dog!

Varro's Servant
How dost, fool?

How are you, fool?

APEMANTUS
Dost dialogue with thy shadow?

Are you talking to your shadow?

Varro's Servant
I speak not to thee.

I wasn't talking to you.

APEMANTUS
No,'tis to thyself.
To the Fool
Come away.

No, you were talking to yourself.
[to the Fool]
Come away.

Isidore's Servant
There's the fool hangs on your back already.

There's the fool hanging on your back already.

APEMANTUS
No, thou stand'st single, thou'rt not on him yet.

No, you're standing alone, you're not there yet.

CAPHIS
Where's the fool now?

Where's the fool now?

APEMANTUS
He last asked the question. Poor rogues, and usurers' men! bawds between gold and want!

He's the one who asked the last question. Poor scoundrels, moneylenders' men! Pimps between money and need!

All Servants
What are we, Apemantus?

What are we, Apemantus?

APEMANTUS
Asses.

Asses.

All Servants
Why?

Why?

APEMANTUS
That you ask me what you are, and do not know yourselves. Speak to 'em, fool.

Because you ask me what you are, and don't know yourselves. Speak to them, fool.

Fool
How do you, gentlemen?

How are you, gentlemen?

All Servants
Gramercies, good fool: how does your mistress?

Well, thanks, good fool; how is your mistress?

Fool

She's e'en setting on water to scald such chickens
as you are. Would we could see you at Corinth!

She's just boiling the water to pluck chickens like you. If only we could see you in Corinth!

APEMANTUS

Good! gramercy.

Very good! Praise God.

Enter Page

Fool

Look you, here comes my mistress' page.

Look, here comes my mistress' page.

Page

[To the Fool] Why, how now, captain! what do you
in this wise company? How dost thou,
Apemantus?

Why, hello there, captain! What are you doing amongst all these wise people? How are you, Apemantus?

APEMANTUS

Would I had a rod in my mouth, that I might answer
thee profitably.

I wish I had a cane instead of a tongue, to give you a proper lashing.

Page

Prithee, Apemantus, read me the superscription of
these letters: I know not which is which.

Please, Apemantus, read the addresses on these letters for me: I don't know which is which.

APEMANTUS

Canst not read?

Can't you read?

Page

No.

No.

APEMANTUS

There will little learning die then, that day thou art hanged. This is to Lord Timon; this to Alcibiades. Go; thou wast born a bastard, and thou't
die a bawd.

Not much learning will die then, the day you're hanged. This one's for Lord Timon; this for Alcibiades. Go; you were born a bastard, and you'll die a pimp.

Page

Thou wast whelped a dog, and thou shalt famish a
dog's death. Answer not; I am gone.

You're a son of a bitch, and you'll die as a starving dog. Don't answer me, I'm gone.

Exit

APEMANTUS
E'en so thou outrunnest grace. Fool, I will go with
you to Lord Timon's.

This is just how you run away from salvation. Fool,
I will go with you to Lord Timon's.

Fool
Will you leave me there?

Are you going to leave me there?

APEMANTUS
If Timon stay at home. You three serve three usurers?

If Timon stays at home. You three work for moneylenders?

All Servants
Ay; would they served us!

Yes, we wish they worked for us!

APEMANTUS
So would I,--as good a trick as ever hangman served thief.

I wish that too - that they'd work the trick on you the hangman
works on the thief.

Fool
Are you three usurers' men?

Are you three moneylenders' men?

All Servants
Ay, fool.

Yes, fool.

Fool
I think no usurer but has a fool to his servant: my
mistress is one, and I am her fool. When men come
to borrow of your masters, they approach sadly, and
go away merry; but they enter my mistress' house
merrily, and go away sadly: the reason of this?

I think all moneylenders have fools as servants; my
mistress is one, and I am her fool. When men come
to borrow from your masters, they come sad and
leave merry; but they come to my mistress's house merry
and go away sad. Why is this?

Varro's Servant
I could render one.

I can think of a reason.

APEMANTUS
Do it then, that we may account thee a whoremaster
and a knave; which not-withstanding, thou shalt
be no less esteemed.

Tell us then, so we can say you are a pimp and a knave;
we won't think any less of you for it.

Varro's Servant
What is a whoremaster, fool?

What's a pimp, fool?

Fool
A fool in good clothes, and something like thee.
'Tis a spirit: sometime't appears like a lord;
sometime like a lawyer; sometime like a
philosopher,
with two stones moe than's artificial one: he is
very often like a knight; and, generally, in all
shapes that man goes up and down in from
fourscore
to thirteen, this spirit walks in.

A fool in a nice suit, a bit like you.
He's a ghost; sometimes he looks like a lord;
sometimes a lawyer; sometimes a philosopher,
with two stones more than his scientific one:
he's
very often like a knight; and, overall, he takes
on
all the shapes men assume between thirteen
and eighty.

Varro's Servant
Thou art not altogether a fool.

You're not a complete fool.

Fool
Nor thou altogether a wise man: as much
foolery as
I have, so much wit thou lackest.

Nor are you a completely wise man: for all the
foolery I have,
you're missing the same amount of wit.

APEMANTUS
That answer might have become Apemantus.

That answer could have come from me.

All Servants
Aside, aside; here comes Lord Timon.

Stand aside; here comes Lord Timon.

Re-enter TIMON and FLAVIUS

APEMANTUS
Come with me, fool, come.

Come with me, fool, come.

Fool
I do not always follow lover, elder brother and
woman; sometime the philosopher.

I don't always follow a lover, elder brother or
woman; sometimes I follow a philosopher.

Exeunt APEMANTUS and Fool

FLAVIUS
Pray you, walk near: I'll speak with you anon.

Please, stay nearby: I'll speak to you shortly.

Exeunt Servants

TIMON
You make me marvel: wherefore ere this time

You astonish me: why didn't you explain

Had you not fully laid my state before me,
That I might so have rated my expense,
As I had leave of means?

FLAVIUS
You would not hear me,
At many leisures I proposed.

TIMON
Go to:
Perchance some single vantages you took.
When my indisposition put you back:
And that unaptness made your minister,
Thus to excuse yourself.

FLAVIUS
O my good lord,
At many times I brought in my accounts,
Laid them before you; you would throw them off,
And say, you found them in mine honesty.
When, for some trifling present, you have bid me
Return so much, I have shook my head and wept;
Yea, 'gainst the authority of manners, pray'd you
To hold your hand more close: I did endure
Not seldom, nor no slight cheques, when I have
Prompted you in the ebb of your estate
And your great flow of debts. My loved lord,
Though you hear now, too late--yet now's a time--
The greatest of your having lacks a half
To pay your present debts.

TIMON
Let all my land be sold.

FLAVIUS
'Tis all engaged, some forfeited and gone;
And what remains will hardly stop the mouth
Of present dues: the future comes apace:
What shall defend the interim? and at length
How goes our reckoning?

the state of my affairs earlier,
so I could have suited my expenditure
to my means?

You wouldn't listen,
I suggested it many times.

Come on:
maybe you tried occasionally,
when I didn't have time to listen,
and you made my unavailability
your excuse not to try again.

Oh my good lord,
many times I brought in my accounts,
and put them in front of you; you would push them away,
and say you trusted my honesty.
When you have told me to give so much in return
for some little present I have shaken my head and wept;
in contradiction to the laws of manners I begged you
to be less extravagant; I had to put up with frequent harsh rebukes, when I
told you how your estate was running out of money, and how much debt you were piling up.
My beloved lord, though you're listening now it's too late - but I must still tell you -
everything you've got won't pay half
of the debts you have.

Let all my land be sold.

It's all mortgaged, some of it forfeited and gone
for good; and what there is left will hardly cover the debts
due now; the future's rushing on us:
how shall we live for now? And what's our long term plan?

TIMON

To Lacedaemon did my land extend.

My lands stretched as far as Lacedaemon.

FLAVIUS

O my good lord, the world is but a word:
Were it all yours to give it in a breath,
How quickly were it gone!

Oh my good lord, the world is just a word:
if it was all yours to give away in one breath,
how quickly it would be gone.

TIMON

You tell me true.

You're right.

FLAVIUS

If you suspect my husbandry or falsehood,
Call me before the exactest auditors
And set me on the proof. So the gods bless me,
When all our offices have been oppress'd
With riotous feeders, when our vaults have
wept
With drunken spilth of wine, when every room
Hath blazed with lights and bray'd with
minstrelsy,
I have retired me to a wasteful cock,
And set mine eyes at flow.

If you suspect me of bad accounting or fraud,
call in the strictest auditors
and ask me to prove myself. I swear by the
gods, that when all we servants have been
overwhelmed with rowdy feasters, when our
cellars have been swamped
with drunkenly spilled wine, when every room
has blazed with lights and been packed with
musicians,
I have gone down to the swimming cellars,
and added my tears to the flow of wine.

TIMON

Prithee, no more.

Please, no more.

FLAVIUS

Heavens, have I said, the bounty of this lord!
How many prodigal bits have slaves and
peasants
This night englutted! Who is not Timon's?
What heart, head, sword, force, means, but is
Lord Timon's?
Great Timon, noble, worthy, royal Timon!
Ah, when the means are gone that buy this
praise,
The breath is gone whereof this praise is made:
Feast-won, fast-lost; one cloud of winter
showers,
These flies are couch'd.

Heavens, I've said to myself, the generosity of
this lord! how much extravagant food slaves
and peasants have
gobbled tonight! Who doesn't love Timon?
What heart, head, strength, money, isn't
devoted to
Lord Timon?
Great Timon, noble, worthy, royal Timon!
Ah, when the money to buy this praise is gone,
the breath that formed this praise is gone too:
won with feasting, lost with hunger; if there's
one cloud
bringing winter showers, these flies leave.

TIMON

Come, sermon me no further:
No villanous bounty yet hath pass'd my heart;
Unwisely, not ignobly, have I given.

Come, stop lecturing me:
I've never done anything that supported evil;
I've given unwisely, not dishonourably.

Why dost thou weep? Canst thou the conscience lack,
To think I shall lack friends? Secure thy heart;
If I would broach the vessels of my love,
And try the argument of hearts by borrowing,
Men and men's fortunes could I frankly use
As I can bid thee speak.

Why are you weeping? Do you really believe that I will lack friends? Don't worry; if I was to open up these people's hearts, and put all their promises to the test, I could get them to serve me, as easily as I can ask you to speak.

FLAVIUS
Assurance bless your thoughts!

I hope this will prove true!

TIMON
And, in some sort, these wants of mine are crown'd,
That I account them blessings; for by these
Shall I try friends: you shall perceive how you
Mistake my fortunes; I am wealthy in my friends.
Within there! Flaminius! Servilius!

And in some ways these problems are a good thing, I'll call them a blessing; this is the way I shall see who my friends are: you shall see that you're wrong to think I am poor; I am rich in friends. Hello there! Flaminius! Servillus!

Enter FLAMINIUS, SERVILIUS, and other Servants

Servants
My lord? my lord?

My lord? My lord?

TIMON
I will dispatch you severally; you to Lord Lucius;
to Lord Lucullus you: I hunted with his honour to-day: you, to Sempronius: commend me to their
loves, and, I am proud, say, that my occasions have
found time to use 'em toward a supply of money: let
the request be fifty talents.

I'll send you off to different places; you go to Lord Luciius; you to Lord Lucullus: I hunted with his honour today: you go to Sempronius: give them my compliments and say, I am proud, that I have found myself in need of some cash-flow: ask them for fifty talents.

FLAMINIUS
As you have said, my lord.

Just as you say, my lord.

FLAVIUS
[Aside] Lord Lucius and Lucullus? hum!

Lords Lucius and Lucullus? Hmm!

TIMON
Go you, sir, to the senators--

You, sir, go to the senators-

Of whom, even to the state's best health, I have
Deserved this hearing--bid 'em send o' the instant
A thousand talents to me.

FLAVIUS
I have been bold--
For that I knew it the most general way--
To them to use your signet and your name;
But they do shake their heads, and I am here
No richer in return.

TIMON
Is't true? can't be?

FLAVIUS
They answer, in a joint and corporate voice,
That now they are at fall, want treasure, cannot
Do what they would; are sorry--you are honourable,--
But yet they could have wish'd--they know not--
Something hath been amiss--a noble nature
May catch a wrench--would all were well--'tis pity;--
And so, intending other serious matters,
After distasteful looks and these hard fractions,
With certain half-caps and cold-moving nods
They froze me into silence.

TIMON
You gods, reward them!
Prithee, man, look cheerly. These old fellows
Have their ingratitude in them hereditary:
Their blood is caked, 'tis cold, it seldom flows;
'Tis lack of kindly warmth they are not kind;
And nature, as it grows again toward earth,
Is fashion'd for the journey, dull and heavy.

To a Servant
Go to Ventidius.

To FLAVIUS
Prithee, be not sad,
Thou art true and honest; ingeniously I speak.
No blame belongs to thee.

because of what I have done for the state, I deserve
their attention - tell them to send me
a thousand talents at once.

I took the liberty-
for I knew it was our best bet-
to use your credentials to ask them;
but they shook their heads, and here I am,
no richer than before.

Is this true? Can this really have happened?

They said unanimously
that they are at a low ebb, they lack money and can't
do as they'd like to; they are sorry-they know you're a good man-
but they wish you- they don't know-
something was wrong-a noble man
can go off the rails-they wished all was well-it was a shame-
and so, moving on to other important matters,
after looking disdainful and giving me these harsh words, with a wave of the hand and a chilly nod, they dismissed me.

You gods, give them what they deserve!
Come on man, cheer up. These old fellows are always mean, it comes with age:
their blood is thick, it's cold, they have no passion; lacking kindly warmth they are not kind; and nature, as it starts back towards the earth it came from, begins to suit itself to the journey, becomes dull and heavy.

Go to Ventidius.

Please, don't be sad,
you are faithful and honest; I'm speaking honestly. There's no blame on you.

48

To Servant
Ventidius lately
Buried his father; by whose death he's stepp'd
Into a great estate: when he was poor,
Imprison'd and in scarcity of friends,
I clear'd him with five talents: greet him from me;
Bid him suppose some good necessity
Touches his friend, which craves to be remember'd
With those five talents.

Ventidius recently buried his father; through his death he's acquired a large fortune: when he was poor, imprisoned and lacking friends, I paid his debts with five talents: give him my regards, and inform him that his friend is in genuine need, and he would appreciate him returning the favour with those five talents.

Exit Servant

To FLAVIUS
That had, give't these fellows
To whom 'tis instant due. Ne'er speak, or think,
That Timon's fortunes 'mong his friends can sink.

Once we have that, pay off those fellows who are claiming it at once. Never say or think that Timon will lose his friends.

FLAVIUS
I would I could not think it: that thought is bounty's foe;
Being free itself, it thinks all others so.

I wish I couldn't think it; thinking that makes it easy for you to be exploited; when you're generous, you tend to think everyone else is the same.

Exeunt

Act 3

SCENE I. A room in Lucullus' house.

FLAMINIUS waiting. Enter a Servant to him

Servant
I have told my lord of you; he is coming down
to you.

*I've told my lord you're here; he's coming down
to you.*

FLAMINIUS
I thank you, sir.

Thank you, sir.

Enter LUCULLUS

Servant
Here's my lord.

Here's my lord.

LUCULLUS
[Aside] One of Lord Timon's men? a gift, I
warrant. Why, this hits right; I dreamt of a
silver
basin and ewer to-night. Flaminius, honest
Flaminius; you are very respectively welcome,
sir.
Fill me some wine.

*One of Timon's men? Bringing a gift,
I bet. Why, this all fits; I dreamt of a silver
basin and jug tonight. Flaminius, honest
Flaminius; you are respectfully welcome, sir.
get some wine.*

Exit Servants

And how does that honourable, complete, free-
hearted
gentleman of Athens, thy very bountiful good
lord
and master?

*And how is that honourable, open hearted,
complete
gentleman of Athens, your generous lord
and master?*

FLAMINIUS
His health is well sir.

He's in good health, sir.

LUCULLUS
I am right glad that his health is well, sir: and
what hast thou there under thy cloak, pretty
Flaminius?

*I'm very glad to hear it, sir; and
what are you hiding under your cloak, sweet
Flaminius?*

FLAMINIUS
'Faith, nothing but an empty box, sir; which, in
my
lord's behalf, I come to entreat your honour to
supply; who, having great and instant occasion

*I swear, nothing but an empty box, sir; which,
on
behalf of my master, I have come to beg your
honour to fill;*

to
use fifty talents, hath sent to your lordship to
furnish him, nothing doubting your present
assistance therein.

LUCULLUS
La, la, la, la! 'nothing doubting,' says he? Alas,
good lord! a noble gentleman 'tis, if he would
not
keep so good a house. Many a time and often I
ha'
dined with him, and told him on't, and come
again to
supper to him, of purpose to have him spend
less,
and yet he would embrace no counsel, take no
warning
by my coming. Every man has his fault, and
honesty
is his: I ha' told him on't, but I could ne'er get
him from't.

Re-enter Servant, with wine

Servant
Please your lordship, here is the wine.

LUCULLUS
Flaminius, I have noted thee always wise.
Here's to thee.

FLAMINIUS
Your lordship speaks your pleasure.

LUCULLUS
I have observed thee always for a towardly
prompt
spirit--give thee thy due--and one that knows
what
belongs to reason; and canst use the time well,
if
the time use thee well: good parts in thee.

To Servant
Get you gone, sirrah.

*he has urgent need of fifty talents at once, and he's
sent me to you to ask for them, having no doubt
that you will help him out.*

*Tra la la! 'Having no doubt,' he says? Alas,
good lord! He would be a noble gentleman,
if he wasn't so profligate. Many times I have
dined with him, and spoken to him about it, and
again
come to supper with him, telling him to spend
less,
but he would not take any advice, he wouldn't
be warned
by my visits. Every man has his faults, and
over-generosity
is his: I warned him about it, but I couldn't ever
dissuade him.*

If you please, your lordship, here is the wine.

*Flaminius, I've always respected your wisdom.
Here's to you.*

Your lordship is kind to say so.

*I have always seen you as a friendly and well
disposed chap
- to give you your due-and someone with plenty
of common sense; and you can do well, if
luck favours you; you have good qualities.*

*[to servant]
Off you go, sir.*

Exit Servant

Draw nearer, honest Flaminius. Thy lord's a
bountiful gentleman: but thou art wise; and
thou
knowest well enough, although thou comest to
me,
that this is no time to lend money, especially
upon
bare friendship, without security. Here's three
solidares for thee: good boy, wink at me, and
say
thou sawest me not. Fare thee well.

*Come closer, honest Flaminius. Your lord is a
generous
gentleman: but you are wise; and you
know well enough, although you've come to me,
that this is not a good time to be lending money,
without security, just on the basis of friendship.
Here are
three shillings for you; look the other way,
and say you didn't see me. Farewell.*

FLAMINIUS
Is't possible the world should so much differ,
And we alive that lived? Fly, damned baseness,
To him that worships thee!

*Is it possible for the world to change so much
in the span of a single lifetime? You filthy stuff,
go back to the one who worships you!*

Throwing the money back

LUCULLUS
Ha! now I see thou art a fool, and fit for thy
master.

*Ha! I see now that you're a fool, and well
suited to your master.*

Exit

FLAMINIUS
May these add to the number that may scald
thee!
Let moulten coin be thy damnation,
Thou disease of a friend, and not himself!
Has friendship such a faint and milky heart,
It turns in less than two nights? O you gods,
I feel master's passion! this slave,
Unto his honour, has my lord's meat in him:
Why should it thrive and turn to nutriment,
When he is turn'd to poison?
O, may diseases only work upon't!
And, when he's sick to death, let not that part of
nature
Which my lord paid for, be of any power
To expel sickness, but prolong his hour!

*May these be added to the collection which
burn you!
Let melted coins be your torture in hell,
you disease of friendship, no true friend!
Is friendship so weak and insipid
that it changes in less than two nights? Oh you
gods, I feel the anger my master would! This
slave, who pretends to be so honourable, is full
of my lord's food:
why should it nourish him,
when he is so poisonous?
Oh, may it only bring him diseases!
And, when he's sick to death, don't let any part
of his body
which grew through my lordship's food help
to cure him, let it prolong his agony!*

Exit

SCENE II. A public place.

Enter LUCILIUS, with three Strangers

LUCILIUS
Who, the Lord Timon? he is my very good friend, and
an honourable gentleman.

Who, Lord Timon? He's a very good friend of mine,
and an honourable gentleman.

First Stranger
We know him for no less, though we are but strangers
to him. But I can tell you one thing, my lord, and
which I hear from common rumours: now Lord Timon's
happy hours are done and past, and his estate shrinks from him.

That's what we think of him too, although we are unknown
to him. But I can tell you one thing, my lord, which
everyone is talking about: now Lord Timon's good times are over, and he's losing his fortune.

LUCILIUS
Fie, no, do not believe it; he cannot want for money.

Nonsense, don't believe it; he can't need money.

Second Stranger
But believe you this, my lord, that, not long ago,
one of his men was with the Lord Lucullus to borrow
so many talents, nay, urged extremely for't and showed what necessity belonged to't, and yet was denied.

But you should know this, my lord, that, not long ago,
one of his men went to the Lord Lucullus to borrow
some talents, indeed he was very pressing and said the matter was extremely urgent, but he was refused.

LUCILIUS
How!

What!

Second Stranger
I tell you, denied, my lord.

I tell you, he was refused, my lord.

LUCILIUS
What a strange case was that! now, before the gods,
I am ashamed on't. Denied that honourable man!
there was very little honour showed in't. For my own
part, I must needs confess, I have received

What a peculiar business that is! I swear to the gods,
it makes me ashamed. Refused that honourable man?
That was a dishonourable act. On my own part, I must admit I have had some little presents from him, like money, plate,

some
small kindnesses from him, as money, plate, jewels
and such-like trifles, nothing comparing to his;
yet, had he mistook him and sent to me, I should
ne'er have denied his occasion so many talents.

jewels
and similar trinkets, nothing like his ones;
but, if he had mistakenly sent the request to me, I would
never have refused him a sum of talents in his need.

Enter SERVILIUS

SERVILIUS
See, by good hap, yonder's my lord;
I have sweat to see his honour. My honoured lord,--

See, luckily, my lord is over there;
I need to see him urgently. My honoured lord—

LUCILIUS
Servilius! you are kindly met, sir. Fare thee well:
commend me to thy honourable virtuous lord, my very
exquisite friend.

Servilius! It's good to see you, sir. Farewell:
give my regards to your honourable virtuous lord,
my most delightful friend.

SERVILIUS
May it please your honour, my lord hath sent--

If you please your honour, my lord has sent—

LUCILIUS
Ha! what has he sent? I am so much endeared to
that lord; he's ever sending: how shall I thank him, thinkest thou? And what has he sent now?

Ha! What has he sent? I am so grateful to that lord,
he's always sending things: how do you think I should thank him? What has he sent this time?

SERVILIUS
Has only sent his present occasion now, my lord;
requesting your lordship to supply his instant use
with so many talents.

All he has sent today is news of his need, my lord;
he asks your lordship to help his immediate wants
by giving him a number of talents.

Lucilius
I know his lordship is but merry with me;
He cannot want fifty five hundred talents.

I know his Lordship is only having a joke with me; however big a sum was he could always cover it.

SERVILIUS
But in the mean time he wants less, my lord.
If his occasion were not virtuous,
I should not urge it half so faithfully.

But at the moment he doesn't want a large sum, my lord. If his needs hadn't been honestly incurred, I wouldn't be half as keen to ask.

LUCILIUS
Dost thou speak seriously, Servilius?

Are you being serious, Servilius?

SERVILIUS
Upon my soul,'tis true, sir.

I swear, it's true, sir.

LUCILIUS
What a wicked beast was I to disfurnish myself
against such a good time, when I might ha'
shown
myself honourable! how unluckily it happened,
that I
should purchase the day before for a little part,
and undo a great deal of honoured! Servilius,
now,
before the gods, I am not able to do,--the more
beast, I say:--I was sending to use Lord Timon
myself, these gentlemen can witness! but I
would
not, for the wealth of Athens, I had done't now.
Commend me bountifully to his good lordship;
and I
hope his honour will conceive the fairest of me,
because I have no power to be kind: and tell
him
this from me, I count it one of my greatest
afflictions, say, that I cannot pleasure such an
honourable gentleman. Good Servilius, will you
befriend me so far, as to use mine own words to
him?

*How wrong of me not to have prepared myself
properly for this fortunate occasion, when I
could have shown
myself to be honourable! How unfortunate that
just yesterday I invested my money in a little
business, which means I can't do something so
honourable! Servilius,
I swear that I can't help you (I'm a real beast, I
say!)
—I was about to send to Lord Timon myself to
borrow money,
these gentlemen can witness it—I would give the
wealth
of Athens not to have done it. Give his good
lordship
my warmest regards; and I hope his
honour will think the best of me, because I can't
possibly help him: and tell him
from me, that it is a source of enormous
regret that I can't help such an
honourable gentleman. Good Servilius, will you
do me the favour of using my own words to
him?*

SERVILIUS
Yes, sir, I shall.

Yes, sir, I shall.

LUCILIUS
I'll look you out a good turn, Servilius.

*I'll have to think of something I can do the you,
Servilius.*

Exit SERVILIUS

True as you said, Timon is shrunk indeed;
And he that's once denied will hardly speed.

*It's just as you said, Timon has come down;
and once you fall you can't get back up.*

Exit

First Stranger
Do you observe this, Hostilius?

Do you see this, Hostilius?

Second Stranger
Ay, too well.

Yes, all too well.

First Stranger
Why, this is the world's soul; and just of the same piece
Is every flatterer's spirit. Who can call him
His friend that dips in the same dish? for, in
My knowing, Timon has been this lord's father,
And kept his credit with his purse,
Supported his estate; nay, Timon's money
Has paid his men their wages: he ne'er drinks,
But Timon's silver treads upon his lip;
And yet--O, see the monstrousness of man
When he looks out in an ungrateful shape!--
He does deny him, in respect of his,
What charitable men afford to beggars.

*Why, this is the way the world works; and every
flatterer has the same character. Who can call
someone a friend just because he shares a
meal? To my knowledge, Timon has been like a
father to this lord, maintained his credit with
his own money, supported his establishment;
why, Timon's money
has paid his servants' wages: he never drinks
without it being from a silver cup of Timon's;
and yet–oh, see how monstrous men are when
they become ungrateful!
He is refusing him something which, in
proportion,
is just what a kind man would give to a beggar.*

Third Stranger
Religion groans at it.

The gods despair at it.

First Stranger
For mine own part,
I never tasted Timon in my life,
Nor came any of his bounties over me,
To mark me for his friend; yet, I protest,
For his right noble mind, illustrious virtue
And honourable carriage,
Had his necessity made use of me,
I would have put my wealth into donation,
And the best half should have return'd to him,
So much I love his heart: but, I perceive,
Men must learn now with pity to dispense;
For policy sits above conscience.

*On my part,
I've never had any experience of Timon,
and never have I had any of his largess
to make me his friend; but, I swear,
for his very noble mind, shining virtues
and honourable conduct,
if he had applied to me in his hour of need,
I would have regarded my wealth as his gift,
and would have sent more than half back to
him, that's how much I admire him: but, I see,
men must now learn to be pitiless;
desires triumph over conscience.*

Exeunt

SCENE III. A room in Sempronius' house.

Enter SEMPRONIUS, and a Servant of TIMON's

SEMPRONIUS
Must he needs trouble me in 't,--hum!--'bove
all others?
He might have tried Lord Lucius or Lucullus;
And now Ventidius is wealthy too,
Whom he redeem'd from prison: all these
Owe their estates unto him.

Servant
My lord,
They have all been touch'd and found base
metal, for
They have all denied him.

SEMPRONIUS
How! have they denied him?
Has Ventidius and Lucullus denied him?
And does he send to me? Three? hum!
It shows but little love or judgment in him:
Must I be his last refuge! His friends, like
physicians,
Thrive, give him over: must I take the cure
upon me?
Has much disgraced me in't; I'm angry at him,
That might have known my place: I see no
sense for't,
But his occasion might have woo'd me first;
For, in my conscience, I was the first man
That e'er received gift from him:
And does he think so backwardly of me now,
That I'll requite its last? No:
So it may prove an argument of laughter
To the rest, and 'mongst lords I be thought a
fool.
I'ld rather than the worth of thrice the sum,
Had sent to me first, but for my mind's sake;
I'd such a courage to do him good. But now
return,
And with their faint reply this answer join;
Who bates mine honour shall not know my
coin.

58

Does he need to bother me about it–hmph!–
more than anyone else?
He might have tried Lord Lucius or Lucullus;
and now Ventidius is wealthy too,
and he got him out of prison; all of them
owe their wealth to him.

My lord,
they have all been tried and found to be false,
they have all turned him down.

What? Have they refused him?
Have Ventidius and Lucullus refused him?
And he's sent to me? Three of them? Eh?
This shows he doesn't have much love always
done.
Am I to be his last resort? His friends who have
done well
on his money give up on him; do I have to sort
it all out?
This is a great insult to me; I'm angry with him,
I should have been top of his list. I can't see
why
he didn't ask me first when he was in need:
for, to the best of my belief, I was the first man
that ever got a gift from him.
And does he think so little of me now
that I'm the last person he asks? No:
this way all the rest will laugh
at me, and the lords will think I'm a fool.
I would pay three times the sum he mentions
to have him ask me first, just because of my
liking for him;
I was so keen to help him. But now send back to
him and add this answer to the unsupportive
ones he already has:
if you insult my honour you won't get my
money.

Exit

Servant

Excellent! Your lordship's a goodly villain. The devil knew not what he did when he made man politic; he crossed himself by 't: and I cannot think but, in the end, the villainies of man will set him clear. How fairly this lord strives to appear foul! takes virtuous copies to be wicked, like those that under hot ardent zeal would set whole realms on fire: Of such a nature is his politic love.
This was my lord's best hope; now all are fled,
Save only the gods: now his friends are dead,
Doors, that were ne'er acquainted with their wards
Many a bounteous year must be employ'd
Now to guard sure their master.
And this is all a liberal course allows;
Who cannot keep his wealth must keep his house.

Excellent! Your lordship is a proper villain. The devil didn't know what he was doing when he made men cunning; he did himself a bad turn: and I can only think that, in the end, the villainy of mankind will triumph. What a good job this lord does of looking innocent when being evil! He imitates a virtuous man in order to be wicked, like those religious types who are willing for whole countries to suffer for their faith: this is what his cunning love is like.
This was my lord's best chance; now everyone but the gods have given up on him: now he has no friends, doors that were always open to him before in the good times will now be used to keep their master locked away. This is all that generosity gets you; you end up hiding in your house from your creditors.

Exit

60

SCENE IV. The same. A hall in Timon's house.

Enter two Servants of Varro, and the Servant of LUCIUS, meeting TITUS, HORTENSIUS, and other Servants of TIMON's creditors, waiting his coming out

Lucilius' Servant
Not yet.

Varro's First Servant
Well met; good morrow, Titus and Hortensius.

TITUS
The like to you kind Varro.

HORTENSIUS
Lucius!
What, do we meet together?

Lucilius' Servant
Ay, and I think
One business does command us all; for mine is
money.

TITUS
So is theirs and ours.

Enter PHILOTUS

Lucilius' Servant
And Sir Philotus too!

PHILOTUS
Good day at once.

Lucilius' Servant
Welcome, good brother.
What do you think the hour?

PHILOTUS
Labouring for nine.

Lucilius' Servant
So much?

PHILOTUS
Is not my lord seen yet?

Good day to you, Titus and Hortensius.

The same to you, kind Varro.

Lucius!
Both here once, are we?

Yes, and I think
we're all here on the same business; I'm here
for money.

So are we and so are they.

And here's Sir Philotus as well!

Good day to you all.

Welcome, good brother.
What time is it?

It's getting on towards nine.

As late as that?

Hasn't he been out yet?

Not yet.

PHILOTUS
I wonder on't; he was wont to shine at seven.

I'm surprised; he used to come out at seven.

Lucilius' Servant
Ay, but the days are wax'd shorter with him:
You must consider that a prodigal course
Is like the sun's; but not, like his, recoverable.
I fear 'tis deepest winter in Lord Timon's purse;
That is one may reach deep enough, and yet
Find little.

*Yes, but his days have grown shorter now:
you must think that the life of the profligate
man is like the orbit of the sun; but unlike the
sun he doesn't return after he has set.
I'm afraid it's deepest winter in Lord Timon's
purse; one can reach as deep as one wants, but
you won't find anything.*

PHILOTUS
I am of your fear for that.

That's what I'm afraid of.

TITUS
I'll show you how to observe a strange event.
Your lord sends now for money.

*I'll tell you how to interpret an odd business.
Your lord has sent you for money.*

HORTENSIUS
Most true, he does.

Very true, he has.

TITUS
And he wears jewels now of Timon's gift,
For which I wait for money.

*And he's wearing jewels which Timon gave
him,
which is the reason he can't afford to pay me.*

HORTENSIUS
It is against my heart.

It grieves me.

Lucilius' Servant
Mark, how strange it shows,
Timon in this should pay more than he owes:
And e'en as if your lord should wear rich
jewels,
And send for money for 'em.

*Look how odd it is,
Timon is having to pay more than he owes:
he's given your lord the sum in rich jewels,
and now he's asking for the money as well.*

HORTENSIUS
I'm weary of this charge, the gods can witness:
I know my lord hath spent of Timon's wealth,
And now ingratitude makes it worse than
stealth.

*I'm fed up with this job, I swear to the gods:
I know my lord spent Timon's money,
and now his ingratitude makes it worse than
stealing.*

Varro's First Servant
Yes, mine's three thousand crowns: what's
yours?

*Yes, mine's after three thousand crowns: what
about yours?*

Lucilius' Servant

Five thousand mine.

Mine wants five thousand.

Varro's First Servant
'Tis much deep: and it should seem by the sun,
Your master's confidence was above mine;
Else, surely, his had equall'd.

It's a large sum: and it would appear
that your master had more confidence than
mine;
otherwise he would surely have lent the same.

Enter FLAMINIUS.

TITUS
One of Lord Timon's men.

Here's one of Lord Timon's men.

Lucilius' Servant
Flaminius! Sir, a word: pray, is my lord ready
to
come forth?

Flaminius! A word with you, sir: tell me, is my
lord
ready to come out?

FLAMINIUS
No, indeed, he is not.

No, he certainly isn't.

TITUS
We attend his lordship; pray, signify so much.

We're waiting for his lordship; please, tell him
so.

FLAMINIUS
I need not tell him that; he knows you are too
diligent.

I don't need to tell him that; he knows how keen
you are.

Exit

Enter FLAVIUS in a cloak, muffled

Lucilius' Servant
Ha! is not that his steward muffled so?
He goes away in a cloud: call him, call him.

Ha! Isn't that his steward all wrapped up?
He's going away in disguise: call him, call him.

TITUS
Do you hear, sir?

Can you hear me, sir?

Varro's Second Servant
By your leave, sir,--

Excuse me, Sir,--

FLAVIUS
What do ye ask of me, my friend?

What you want from me, my friend?

TITUS
We wait for certain money here, sir.

We are waiting here for payment, sir.

FLAVIUS
Ay,
If money were as certain as your waiting,
'Twere sure enough.
Why then preferr'd you not your sums and bills,
When your false masters eat of my lord's meat?
Then they could smile and fawn upon his debts
And take down the interest into their
gluttonous maws.
You do yourselves but wrong to stir me up;
Let me pass quietly:
Believe 't, my lord and I have made an end;
I have no more to reckon, he to spend.

Yes,
if payment was as certain as the fact that you
would wait for it, it would be certain indeed.
Why didn't you come round with your accounts
and bills when your false masters were
enjoying my lord's food? Back then they smiled
and flattered though he owed them, and they
gobbled the price of the interest with their
greedy mouths. You're not doing yourselves any
favours by bothering me; let me go quietly:
believe me, my lord and I finished;
I have no more accounts to add up, he hasn't
any more money to spend.

Lucilius' Servant
Ay, but this answer will not serve.

Yes, but this answer won't serve.

FLAVIUS
If 'twill not serve,'tis not so base as you;
For you serve knaves.

If it won't serve, it's not as bad as you;
because you serve knaves.

Exit

Varro's First Servant
How! what does his cashiered worship mutter?

What's that? What does that jobless lord
mutter?

Varro's Second Servant
No matter what; he's poor, and that's revenge
enough. Who can speak broader than he that
has no
house to put his head in? such may rail against
great buildings.

It doesn't matter what he says; he is poor, and
that's
enough revenge. Someone who has nothing
finds it easy to criticise those who have much.

Enter SERVILIUS

TITUS
O, here's Servilius; now we shall know some
answer.

Oh, here's Servilius; now we shall have some
answers.

SERVILIUS
If I might beseech you, gentlemen, to repair
some
other hour, I should derive much from't; for,
take't of my soul, my lord leans wondrously to
discontent: his comfortable temper has forsook
him;

If I could ask you, gentlemen, to come back
some
other time, I would really appreciate it; for,
I swear to you, my lord has become extremely
depressed: his usual good humour has deserted
him;

he's much out of health, and keeps his chamber.

he's very ill, and is staying in his room.

Lucilius' Servant
Many do keep their chambers are not sick:
And, if it be so far beyond his health,
Methinks he should the sooner pay his debts,
And make a clear way to the gods.

Many stay in their rooms who are not ill:
and, if he's really that ill
I think he ought to pay his debts,
so he'll die with a clear conscience.

SERVILIUS
Good gods!

Good gods!

TITUS
We cannot take this for answer, sir.

We can't accept this as an answer, sir.

FLAMINIUS
[Within] Servilius, help! My lord! my lord!

Servilius, help! My lord! My lord!

Enter TIMON, in a rage, FLAMINIUS following

TIMON
What, are my doors opposed against my passage?
Have I been ever free, and must my house
Be my retentive enemy, my gaol?
The place which I have feasted, does it now,
Like all mankind, show me an iron heart?

What, are my doors locked against my exit?
Have I ever been free, must my house
now become my prison?
The place I used for feasting, does it now,
like all men, show me a hard heart?

Lucilius' Servant
Put in now, Titus.

Put it forward now, Titus.

TITUS
My lord, here is my bill.

My lord, here is my bill.

Lucilius' Servant
Here's mine.

Here's mine.

HORTENSIUS
And mine, my lord.

And mine, my lord.

Both Varro's Servants
And ours, my lord.

And ours, my lord.

PHILOTUS
All our bills.

These are all our bills.

TIMON

Knock me down with 'em: cleave me to the girdle.

Lucilius' Servant
Alas, my lord,-

TIMON
Cut my heart in sums.

TITUS
Mine, fifty talents.

TIMON
Tell out my blood.

Lucilius' Servant
Five thousand crowns, my lord.

TIMON
Five thousand drops pays that.
What yours?--and yours?

Varro's First Servant
My lord,--

Varro's Second Servant
My lord,--

TIMON
Tear me, take me, and the gods fall upon you!

Exit

HORTENSIUS
'Faith, I perceive our masters may throw their caps
at their money: these debts may well be called
desperate ones, for a madman owes 'em.

Exeunt

Re-enter TIMON and FLAVIUS

TIMON
They have e'en put my breath from me, the slaves.

	Knock me down with them: split me in two.
	Alas, my lord,–
	Chop my heart into portions.
	My bill is for fifty talents.
	You can take it out of my blood.
	Five thousand crowns, my lord.
	Five thousand drops would pay for that. What's yours?–And yours?
	My Lord,–
	My Lord,–
	Tear me apart, take the pieces, and may the gods damn you!
	By heaven, I see that our masters can whistle for their money: these debts are certainly irrecoverable, because the money is owed by a madman.
	They've put me quite out of breath, the slaves.

Creditors? devils!

FLAVIUS
My dear lord,--

TIMON
What if it should be so?

FLAVIUS
My lord,--

TIMON
I'll have it so. My steward!

FLAVIUS
Here, my lord.

TIMON
So fitly? Go, bid all my friends again,
Lucius, Lucullus, and Sempronius:
All, sirrah, all:
I'll once more feast the rascals.

FLAVIUS
O my lord,
You only speak from your distracted soul;
There is not so much left, to furnish out
A moderate table.

TIMON
Be't not in thy care; go,
I charge thee, invite them all: let in the tide
Of knaves once more; my cook and I'll provide.

Exeunt

Creditors? Devils!

My dear lord,–

What if I did this?

My lord–

I will do it. Steward!

Here, my lord.

So handy? Go, summon all my friends again,
Lucius, Lucullus and Sempronius:
all of them, sir:
I'll give the rascals another feast.

Oh my lord,
you're only speaking from anguish;
there isn't enough left to lay on
a modest meal.

Don't you worry about that; go,
I order you, invite them all: let the flood
of scoundrels in again; my cook and I will
provide the food.

SCENE V. The same. The senate-house. The Senate sitting.

First Senator
My lord, you have my voice to it; the fault's
Bloody; 'tis necessary he should die:
Nothing emboldens sin so much as mercy.

*My lord, you have my vote; it's a terrible
offence; he has to die for it;
nothing strengthens sin as much as being
merciful.*

Second Senator
Most true; the law shall bruise him.

Very true; the law will crush him.

Enter ALCIBIADES, with Attendants

ALCIBIADES
Honour, health, and compassion to the senate!

*Honour and health to the senate, and may they
be merciful!*

First Senator
Now, captain?

What is it, captain?

ALCIBIADES
I am an humble suitor to your virtues;
For pity is the virtue of the law,
And none but tyrants use it cruelly.
It pleases time and fortune to lie heavy
Upon a friend of mine, who, in hot blood,
Hath stepp'd into the law, which is past depth
To those that, without heed, do plunge into 't.
He is a man, setting his fate aside,
Of comely virtues:
Nor did he soil the fact with cowardice--
An honour in him which buys out his fault--
But with a noble fury and fair spirit,
Seeing his reputation touch'd to death,
He did oppose his foe:
And with such sober and unnoted passion
He did behave his anger, ere 'twas spent,
As if he had but proved an argument.

*I am humbly petitioning your virtues;
for pity is the virtue of the law,
and only tyrants use it cruelly.
Time and fate are heavily oppressing
a friend of mine who, in anger,
has come within the reach of the law,
which is a bottomless pit for those
who slip into it. Apart from this one act
he is a good man.
and he didn't behave badly out of cowardice-
something which forgives his fault-
but with noble anger and a good soul,
seeing his reputation fatally insulted,
he faced his enemy:
he controlled his anger so soberly
that it was as though he was simply making a
point.*

First Senator
You undergo too strict a paradox,
Striving to make an ugly deed look fair:
Your words have took such pains as if they labour'd
To bring manslaughter into form and set quarrelling
Upon the head of valour; which indeed
Is valour misbegot and came into the world

*Your argument doesn't stand up,
as you try to make an ugly deed acceptable:
you talk as if manslaughter was just another
element of discussion, and quarrelling
part of courage; it is in fact
twisted courage, which came into the world
with sects and factions:
the truly brave man tolerates*

When sects and factions were newly born:
He's truly valiant that can wisely suffer
The worst that man can breathe, and make his wrongs
His outsides, to wear them like his raiment, carelessly,
And ne'er prefer his injuries to his heart,
To bring it into danger.
If wrongs be evils and enforce us kill,
What folly 'tis to hazard life for ill!

the worst words men can throw at him,
and wears the insults outside, like his clothes,
and never takes the injuries to heart,
and risks it being injured.
If wrongs are evils that make us kill,
how stupid to risk our lives for them!

ALCIBIADES
My lord,--

My lord -

First Senator
You cannot make gross sins look clear:
To revenge is no valour, but to bear.

You can't make terrible sins seem innocent:
taking revenge isn't bravery, toleration is.

ALCIBIADES
My lords, then, under favour, pardon me,
If I speak like a captain.
Why do fond men expose themselves to battle,
And not endure all threats? sleep upon't,
And let the foes quietly cut their throats,
Without repugnancy? If there be
Such valour in the bearing, what make we
Abroad? why then, women are more valiant
That stay at home, if bearing carry it,
And the ass more captain than the lion, the felon
Loaden with irons wiser than the judge,
If wisdom be in suffering. O my lords,
As you are great, be pitifully good:
Who cannot condemn rashness in cold blood?
To kill, I grant, is sin's extremest gust;
But, in defence, by mercy, 'tis most just.
To be in anger is impiety;
But who is man that is not angry?
Weigh but the crime with this.

Then my lords, by your leave, forgive me
if I speak like a soldier.
Why do foolish men go to war,
instead of putting up with threats? Why don't
they sleep on it
and let the enemies quietly cut their throats
without fighting back? If there is
such bravery in toleration, what are we doing
abroad? Why then, women are braver
for staying at home, bearing it,
and the ass is a braver soldier than the lion,
the criminal in irons is wiser than the judge,
if it is wise to suffer. Oh my lords,
just as you are great, show your goodness
through pity: everyone can condemn a crime
done in cold blood. To kill, I agree, is the worst
of all sins; but in defence, the law mercifully
allows it. To be angry is not pious;
but what man is there who is not angry?
Just think about the crime like that.

Second Senator
You breathe in vain.

You're wasting your breath.

ALCIBIADES
In vain! his service done
At Lacedaemon and Byzantium

Wasting! The service he performed
at Lacedaemon and Byzantium

Were a sufficient briber for his life.

should be enough to save his life.

First Senator
What's that?

What's that?

ALCIBIADES
I say, my lords, he has done fair service,
And slain in fight many of your enemies:
How full of valour did he bear himself
In the last conflict, and made plenteous
wounds!

I'm saying, my lords, he has served you well,
and killed many of your enemies in battle:
how bravely he conducted himself
in the last conflict, and he caused plenty of
wounds!

Second Senator
He has made too much plenty with 'em;
He's a sworn rioter: he has a sin that often
Drowns him, and takes his valour prisoner:
If there were no foes, that were enough
To overcome him: in that beastly fury
He has been known to commit outrages,
And cherish factions: 'tis inferr'd to us,
His days are foul and his drink dangerous.

He has done plenty too much;
he is an habitual drunkard: he has a sin that
often drowns him, and kidnaps his bravery:
if there were no enemies, that sin would be
enough to overcome him: in his drunken fury
he has been known to commit outrages,
and stir up dissent: we have heard it alleged
that he lives a filthy life and is dangerous when
drunk.

First Senator
He dies.

He shall die.

ALCIBIADES
Hard fate! he might have died in war.
My lords, if not for any parts in him--
Though his right arm might purchase his own
time
And be in debt to none--yet, more to move you,
Take my deserts to his, and join 'em both:
And, for I know your reverend ages love
Security, I'll pawn my victories, all
My honours to you, upon his good returns.
If by this crime he owes the law his life,
Why, let the war receive 't in valiant gore
For law is strict, and war is nothing more.

A harsh fate! He might have died in battle.
My lords, if you can't see any good qualities in
him– though his efforts with the sword ought to
be enough to save him on their own–but, to
further persuade you,
add my credit to his, join them together:
and, as I know that in your revered age you
love security, I'll pledge all my victories, all
my honours, that he will make good for you.
If this crime means he owes the law his life,
then let the war take it in bloody bravery,
for the law is strict, and the war is the same.

First Senator
We are for law: he dies; urge it no more,
On height of our displeasure: friend or brother,
He forfeits his own blood that spills another.

We stand for the law: he shall die; stop
arguing, or you will suffer our greatest
displeasure: friend or brother,
if you spill another's blood you lose your own.

ALCIBIADES
Must it be so? it must not be. My lords,

Does it have to be this way? It mustn't be. My

I do beseech you, know me.

lords, I beg you, remember who I am.

Second Senator
How!

What!

ALCIBIADES
Call me to your remembrances.

Remember me.

Third Senator
What!

What!

ALCIBIADES
I cannot think but your age has forgot me;
It could not else be, I should prove so base,
To sue, and be denied such common grace:
My wounds ache at you.

*I can only imagine that you have forgotten me
in your old age; that's the only explanation for
me being so disrespected that I can ask, and be
refused what any man should be given:
my wounds ache to think of it.*

First Senator
Do you dare our anger?
'Tis in few words, but spacious in effect;
We banish thee for ever.

*Do you dare to risk our anger?
I'll give you a few little words, but they'll have a
big effect; we banish you for ever.*

ALCIBIADES
Banish me!
Banish your dotage; banish usury,
That makes the senate ugly.

*Banish me!
Banish your senility, banish moneylending,
that makes the Senate ugly!*

First Senator
If, after two days' shine, Athens contain thee,
Attend our weightier judgment. And, not to
swell
our spirit,
He shall be executed presently.

*If you are still in Athens in two days from now
prepare to get a worse sentence. And, in order
not to
increase our anger,
he shall be executed shortly.*

Exeunt Senators

ALCIBIADES
Now the gods keep you old enough; that you
may live
Only in bone, that none may look on you!
I'm worse than mad: I have kept back their foes,
While they have told their money and let out
Their coin upon large interest, I myself
Rich only in large hurts. All those for this?
Is this the balsam that the usuring senate
Pours into captains' wounds? Banishment!

*Now may the gods make you live so long that
you become
like skeletons, and nobody looks at you!
I'm worse than mad: I kept back their enemies,
while they counted their money, and lent out
their cash at high interest; I myself
am only rich with great wounds. All of those,
for this? Is this the medicine that the
moneylending Senate applies to the wounds of*

It comes not ill; I hate not to be banish'd;
It is a cause worthy my spleen and fury,
That I may strike at Athens. I'll cheer up
My discontented troops, and lay for hearts.
'Tis honour with most lands to be at odds;
Soldiers should brook as little wrongs as gods.

Exit

captains? Banishment! It's no bad thing. I don't hate being banished; it gives me a cause to be angry and attack Athens. I'll rally my discontented troops, and win over people's hearts. One's honour is counted by the number of countries one has fought; soldiers should endure wrongs no more than gods should.

SCENE VI. The same. A banqueting-room in Timon's house.

Music. Tables set out: Servants attending. Enter divers Lords, Senators and others, at several doors

First Lord
The good time of day to you, sir.

A very good day to you, sir.

Second Lord
I also wish it to you. I think this honourable lord
did but try us this other day.

And the same to you. I think this honourable lord
put this before us just the other day.

First Lord
Upon that were my thoughts tiring, when we encountered: I hope it is not so low with him as he made it seem in the trial of his several friends.

I was just musing on that, when we met: I hope he hasn't sunk so low as he made it appear in the trial of some of his friends.

Second Lord
It should not be, by the persuasion of his new feasting.

He shouldn't have, on the evidence of the feasts he's been giving.

First Lord
I should think so: he hath sent me an earnest inviting, which many my near occasions did urge me
to put off; but he hath conjured me beyond them, and
I must needs appear.

I should imagine so: he sent me an earnest invitation, which my many important engagements
made me want to decline; but he begged me so much
that I have to go.

Second Lord
In like manner was I in debt to my importunate business, but he would not hear my excuse. I am
sorry, when he sent to borrow of me, that my provision was out.

In the same way my business was taking up all my time, but he wouldn't listen to my excuse. I am
sorry that when he asked to borrow money from me that I had none to lend him.

First Lord
I am sick of that grief too, as I understand how all
things go.

That made me sad too, especially now I understand
his position.

Second Lord

Every man here's so. What would he have borrowed of you?

74

Every man here thinks the same. What did he want to borrow from you?

First Lord
A thousand pieces.

A thousand gold pieces.

Second Lord
A thousand pieces!

A thousand pieces!

First Lord
What of you?

What about you?

Second Lord
He sent to me, sir,--Here he comes.

He sent to me, sir–here he comes.

Enter TIMON and Attendants

TIMON
With all my heart, gentlemen both; and how
fare you?

*Welcome with all my heart, good gentlemen;
and how are you?*

First Lord
Ever at the best, hearing well of your lordship.

*Always well when we hear your lordship is
well.*

Second Lord
The swallow follows not summer more willing
than we
your lordship.

*The swallow doesn't follow the summer more
willingly than we
follow you.*

TIMON
[Aside] Nor more willingly leaves winter; such
summer-birds are men. Gentlemen, our dinner
will not
recompense this long stay: feast your ears with
the
music awhile, if they will fare so harshly o' the
trumpet's sound; we shall to 't presently.

*Nor is more willing to leave in winter; men are
summer birds. Gentlemen, our dinner will not
be long: feed your ears with the
music for a while, if they can enjoy anything as
harsh
as the trumpet; we'll sit down to dinner shortly.*

First Lord
I hope it remains not unkindly with your
lordship
that I returned you an empty messenger.

*I hope your lordship wasn't offended
that I returned your messenger empty-handed.*

TIMON
O, sir, let it not trouble you.

Oh, sir, don't let it bother you.

Second Lord
My noble lord,--

My noble lord–

TIMON
Ah, my good friend, what cheer?

Ah, my good friend, how are you?

Second Lord
My most honourable lord, I am e'en sick of shame,
that, when your lordship this other day sent to me,
I was so unfortunate a beggar.

My most honourable lord, I am sick with shame that, when your lordship sent me a request the other day,
I was so poor.

TIMON
Think not on 't, sir.

Don't think about it, sir.

Second Lord
If you had sent but two hours before,--

If you had only sent someone two hours before–

TIMON
Let it not cumber your better remembrance.

Don't let it weigh on your mind.

The banquet brought in

Come, bring in all together.

Come on, everyone come in together.

Second Lord
All covered dishes!

All covered dishes!

First Lord
Royal cheer, I warrant you.

Wonderful food, I'll bet.

Third Lord
Doubt not that, if money and the season can yield
it.

You shouldn't doubt it, if money and the season can provide
it.

First Lord
How do you? What's the news?

How are you? What's the news?

Third Lord
Alcibiades is banished: hear you of it?

Alcibiades is banished: did you hear about it?

First Lord Second Lord
Alcibiades banished!

Alcibiades banished!

Third Lord
'Tis so, be sure of it.

Yes, it's definite.

First Lord
How! how!

What! What!

Second Lord
I pray you, upon what?

Tell me, what was the reason?

TIMON
My worthy friends, will you draw near?

My worthy friends, will you come to the table?

Third Lord
I'll tell you more anon. Here's a noble feast toward.

I'll tell you more shortly. There is a great feast to be had.

Second Lord
This is the old man still.

He's like he used to be.

Third Lord
Will 't hold? will 't hold?

Will it last? Can he support it?

Second Lord
It does: but time will--and so--

It does: but time will—and so—

Third Lord
I do conceive.

I understand what you mean.

TIMON
Each man to his stool, with that spur as he would to
the lip of his mistress: your diet shall be in all places alike. Make not a city feast of it, to let the meat cool ere we can agree upon the first place:
sit, sit. The gods require our thanks.
You great benefactors, sprinkle our society with thankfulness. For your own gifts, make yourselves
praised: but reserve still to give, lest your deities be despised. Lend to each man enough, that
one need not lend to another; for, were your godheads to borrow of men, men would forsake the
gods. Make the meat be beloved more than the man
that gives it. Let no assembly of twenty be without

*Every man go to his stool, as keenly as he would to
the lips of his mistress. You shall have the same food at every seat. Don't let's have a formal banquet, where the meat cools
before we can agree who will sit where. Sit, sit. The gods must be thanked.
You great benefactors, sprinkle our company with gratitude.
Allow yourselves to be praised for your gifts; but always keep something in reserve, in case you become hated. Lend each
man enough so that nobody needs to borrow from another; for if your
graces borrowed from men, men would abandon the gods.
Make the meat be more loved than the man who gives it.
Let every company of twenty have twenty villains in it.*

a score of villains: if there sit twelve women at the table, let a dozen of them be--as they are. The rest of your fees, O gods--the senators of Athens, together with the common lag of people--what is amiss in them, you gods, make suitable for destruction. For these my present friends, as they are to me nothing, so in nothing bless them, and to nothing are they welcome. Uncover, dogs, and lap.

If there are twelve women at a table, let a dozen of them be the same. The rest of your property, O gods, the senators of Athens, together with the common people--whatever is wrong with them, you gods, get ready to destroy them. As for these people who are my friends at the moment, as they are nothing to me, so don't bless them in anything, and they are welcome to nothing.
Take off the covers, dogs, and slurp.

The dishes are uncovered and seen to be full of warm water

Some Speak
What does his lordship mean?

What is the meaning of this?

Some Others
I know not.

I don't know.

TIMON
May you a better feast never behold,
You knot of mouth-friends! Smoke and lukewarm water
Is your perfection. This is Timon's last;
Who, stuck and spangled with your flatteries,
Washes it off, and sprinkles in your faces
Your reeking villany.

May you never have a better feast than this, you group of cupboard lovers! Smoke and lukewarm water is all you deserve. This is all Timon has left; sprinkled all over with your flattery, he washes it off, and throws your stinking villainy

Throwing the water in their faces
Live loathed and long,
Most smiling, smooth, detested parasites,
Courteous destroyers, affable wolves, meek bears,
You fools of fortune, trencher-friends, time's flies,
Cap and knee slaves, vapours, and minute-jacks!
Of man and beast the infinite malady
Crust you quite o'er! What, dost thou go?
Soft! take thy physic first--thou too--and thou;--
Stay, I will lend thee money, borrow none.

back in your faces.
Live long hated lives, you smiling, smooth, detestable parasites, polite destroyers, affable wolves, meek bears, you fools of fortune, mealtime friends, summer insects, grovelling slaves, unsubstantial shifters! May the worst illnesses of men and animals scab over your skin! What, are you going? Wait, take your medicine first--you too--and you! Wait, I will lend you money, I won't borrow any.

Throws the dishes at them, and drives them out
What, all in motion? Henceforth be no feast,
Whereat a villain's not a welcome guest.
Burn, house! sink, Athens! henceforth hated be
Of Timon, man and all humanity!

Exit

Re-enter the Lords, Senators, & c

First Lord
How now, my lords!

Second Lord
Know you the quality of Lord Timon's fury?

Third Lord
Push! did you see my cap?

Fourth Lord
I have lost my gown.

First Lord
He's but a mad lord, and nought but humour
sways him.
He gave me a jewel th' other day, and now he
has
beat it out of my hat: did you see my jewel?

Third Lord
Did you see my cap?

Second Lord
Here 'tis.

Fourth Lord
Here lies my gown.

First Lord
Let's make no stay.

Second Lord
Lord Timon's mad.

Third Lord
I feel 't upon my bones.

What? All going? From now on there should be no feast
at which the villain is not a welcome guest.
Burn, house! Sink, Athens! From now on be hated by Timon, man and all humanity!

What's all this, my lords!

Do you know why Lord Timon is so angry?

Tcha! Did you see my cap?

I have lost my gown.

He's just a mad lord, and he is governed by his moods.
He gave me a jewel the other day, and now he has
knocked it out of my hat: did you see my jewel?

Have you seen my cap?

Here it is.

Here is my gown.

Let's not stay here.

Lord Timon is mad.

I can feel that in the bruises he's given me.

Fourth Lord
One day he gives us diamonds, next day stones.   *One day he's throwing diamonds at us, the next day stones.*

Exeunt

Act 4

SCENE I. Without the walls of Athens.

Enter TIMON

TIMON

Let me look back upon thee. O thou wall,
That girdlest in those wolves, dive in the earth,
And fence not Athens! Matrons, turn incontinent!
Obedience fail in children! slaves and fools,
Pluck the grave wrinkled senate from the bench,
And minister in their steads! to general filths
Convert o' the instant, green virginity,
Do 't in your parents' eyes! bankrupts, hold fast;
Rather than render back, out with your knives,
And cut your trusters' throats! bound servants, steal!
Large-handed robbers your grave masters are,
And pill by law. Maid, to thy master's bed;
Thy mistress is o' the brothel! Son of sixteen,
pluck the lined crutch from thy old limping sire,
With it beat out his brains! Piety, and fear,
Religion to the gods, peace, justice, truth,
Domestic awe, night-rest, and neighbourhood,
Instruction, manners, mysteries, and trades,
Degrees, observances, customs, and laws,
Decline to your confounding contraries,
And let confusion live! Plagues, incident to men,
Your potent and infectious fevers heap
On Athens, ripe for stroke! Thou cold sciatica,
Cripple our senators, that their limbs may halt
As lamely as their manners. Lust and liberty
Creep in the minds and marrows of our youth,
That 'gainst the stream of virtue they may strive,
And drown themselves in riot! Itches, blains,
Sow all the Athenian bosoms; and their crop
Be general leprosy! Breath infect breath,
at their society, as their friendship, may
merely poison! Nothing I'll bear from thee,
But nakedness, thou detestable town!
Take thou that too, with multiplying bans!
Timon will to the woods; where he shall find
The unkindest beast more kinder than mankind.

Let me look back at you. Oh you wall
that stretches round those wolves, dive into the earth, and don't protect Athens! Women, be unfaithful!
Children, become disobedient! Slaves and fools, drag the revered wrinkled senators from their benches
and govern in their place! Virgins, turn at once to filthy behaviour!
Do it in front of your parents! Bankrupts, stand firm; instead of repaying your debts, take out your lives, and cut the throats of those who trusted you! Contracted servants, steal!
Your dignified masters are terrible thieves, and they steal legally. Maid, get in your master's bed; your mistress belongs in the brothel! Sixteen-year-old son, grab the padded crutch off your old limping father; beat his brains out with it! Piety and fear, respect for the gods, peace, justice, truth, domestic respect, peace and neighbourliness, teaching, manners, crafts and trades, collapse into your ruinous opposites; and may the destruction continue! Natural plagues of men,
Load your powerful and infectious fevers on Athens, which is ready for them! You cold sciatica, cripple our senators, so that their limbs limp as lamely as their manners! May lust and licentiousness creep into the minds and bones of our youth, so that they fight against everything virtuous, and drown themselves in chaos! Itches, blisters, seed yourself in the bodies of all Athenians, and grow into general leprosy! May each breath infect the other, so that their society, just like their friendship, may be pure poison! I'll carry nothing away from you but my nakedness, you revolting town! Take that too, with multiplied curses! Timon shall go to the woods, where he will find the nastiest beast is kinder than

The gods confound--hear me, you good gods all--
The Athenians both within and out that wall!
And grant, as Timon grows, his hate may grow
To the whole race of mankind, high and low!
Amen.

Exit

mankind. May the gods destroy–hear me, all you good gods– the Athenians, both inside and outside that wall; and allow, as Timon grows, for his hate to grow for the whole race of mankind, high and low!
Amen.

SCENE II. Athens. A room in Timon's house.

Enter FLAVIUS, with two or three Servants

First Servant
Hear you, master steward, where's our master?
Are we undone? cast off? nothing remaining?

FLAVIUS
Alack, my fellows, what should I say to you?
Let me be recorded by the righteous gods,
I am as poor as you.

First Servant
Such a house broke!
So noble a master fall'n! All gone! and not
One friend to take his fortune by the arm,
And go along with him!

Second Servant
As we do turn our backs
From our companion thrown into his grave,
So his familiars to his buried fortunes
Slink all away, leave their false vows with him,
Like empty purses pick'd; and his poor self,
A dedicated beggar to the air,
With his disease of all-shunn'd poverty,
Walks, like contempt, alone. More of our
fellows.

Enter other Servants

FLAVIUS
All broken implements of a ruin'd house.

Third Servant
Yet do our hearts wear Timon's livery;
That see I by our faces; we are fellows still,
Serving alike in sorrow: leak'd is our bark,
And we, poor mates, stand on the dying deck,
Hearing the surges threat: we must all part
Into this sea of air.

FLAVIUS
Good fellows all,
The latest of my wealth I'll share amongst you.

Now then, master steward, where's our master?
Are we finished? Thrown out? Is that it?

Alas, my colleagues, what can I say?
I swear by the just gods,
I am as poor as you.

Such a great household destroyed!
Such a noble master fallen? All gone! And not
one friend to share with him
in his misfortunes!

As we turn away
from the grave of a friend,
so those who loved him when he was rich
sneak away, leaving him their false promises,
like purses that have been robbed; and his poor
self, a homeless beggar,
with his disease of hated poverty,
walks alone, as if he were hatred itself.
Here are more of our colleagues.

All the broken fittings of a ruined house.

But in our hearts we are still Timon's servants;
I can see that in our faces; we are still
colleagues, all serving with the same sorrow;
our ship is holed, and we, poor sailors, stand
on the doomed deck, hearing the waves crash;
we must all leave and wander the world.

You good men,
I'll share the last of my wealth with you.

Wherever we shall meet, for Timon's sake,
Let's yet be fellows; let's shake our heads, and say,
As 'twere a knell unto our master's fortunes,
'We have seen better days.' Let each take some;
Nay, put out all your hands. Not one word more:
Thus part we rich in sorrow, parting poor.

Servants embrace, and part several ways

O, the fierce wretchedness that glory brings us!
Who would not wish to be from wealth exempt,
Since riches point to misery and contempt?
Who would be so mock'd with glory? or to live
But in a dream of friendship?
To have his pomp and all what state compounds
But only painted, like his varnish'd friends?
Poor honest lord, brought low by his own heart,
Undone by goodness! Strange, unusual blood,
When man's worst sin is, he does too much good!
Who, then, dares to be half so kind again?
For bounty, that makes gods, does still mar men.
My dearest lord, bless'd, to be most accursed,
Rich, only to be wretched, thy great fortunes
Are made thy chief afflictions. Alas, kind lord!
He's flung in rage from this ingrateful seat
Of monstrous friends, nor has he with him to
Supply his life, or that which can command it.
I'll follow and inquire him out:
I'll ever serve his mind with my best will;
Whilst I have gold, I'll be his steward still.

Exit

Wherever we may meet, for Timon's sake,
let's still be friends; let's shake our heads and say,
as if we were the funeral bell for our master's fortunes, 'We have seen better days.' Everyone take some; all of you put out your hands. Don't say another word:
so we part, poor but rich in sorrow.

Oh, what excessive wretchedness success brings us! Who wouldn't want to avoid being rich, since riches lead to misery and contempt? Who wants to be mocked by success? Or to live with just the illusion of friendship? To have all his glory and position just a fake, like his deceitful friends? Poor good lord, brought down by his own heart, ruined by goodness! How strange human nature is, when the worst sin a man does is doing too much good! Who will ever dare to be half as generous again? Generosity, which makes the gods, destroys men. My dearest lord, your blessings were a curse, your riches only made you poor, your great fortune has become your greatest burden. Alas, kind lord! He's been thrown out in rage from this ungrateful place of appalling friends, and he hasn't got the necessities of life, or the means to get them. I'll follow and find where he is: I'll always do my best to serve him; while I still have money, I'll still take care of him.

SCENE III. Woods and cave, near the seashore.

Enter TIMON, from the cave

O blessed breeding sun, draw from the earth
Rotten humidity; below thy sister's orb
Infect the air! Twinn'd brothers of one womb,
Whose procreation, residence, and birth,
Scarce is dividant, touch them with several
fortunes;
The greater scorns the lesser: not nature,
To whom all sores lay siege, can bear great
fortune,
But by contempt of nature.
Raise me this beggar, and deny 't that lord;
The senator shall bear contempt hereditary,
The beggar native honour.
It is the pasture lards the rother's sides,
The want that makes him lean. Who dares, who
dares,
In purity of manhood stand upright,
And say 'This man's a flatterer?' if one be,
So are they all; for every grise of fortune
Is smooth'd by that below: the learned pate
Ducks to the golden fool: all is oblique;
There's nothing level in our cursed natures,
But direct villany. Therefore, be abhorr'd
All feasts, societies, and throngs of men!
His semblable, yea, himself, Timon disdains:
Destruction fang mankind! Earth, yield me
roots!

Digging

Who seeks for better of thee, sauce his palate
With thy most operant poison! What is here?
Gold? yellow, glittering, precious gold? No,
gods,
I am no idle votarist: roots, you clear heavens!
Thus much of this will make black white, foul
fair,
Wrong right, base noble, old young, coward
valiant.
Ha, you gods! why this? what this, you gods?
Why, this

Will lug your priests and servants from your
sides,

88

O blessed fertile sun, draw rotting humidity
out of the earth; destroy the land beneath the
moon with infection! Take twin brothers from
the same womb, whose conception, gestation
and birth were almost simultaneous–test them
with several fortunes,
the greater will drive out the lesser. Human
nature, which is constantly under siege from
infection, can't bear great fortune,
except by going against itself.
Raise up this beggar, and deny fortune to that
lord, the senators shall learn what it is to be
looked down on, the beggar what it is to be
exalted. Having pasture is what makes a
brother fat, lack of it makes him thin. Who is
there who dares
to stand up as an honest man
and say, 'This man is a flatterer?' If one is,
they all are, for every step of fortune
is smoothed by what's below: the learned man
bows his head to the rich fool; everything is
immoral; there's nothing straight in our cursed
natures apart from open villainy. So, despise all
feasts, gatherings, and crowds of men!
Timon rejects anything that resembles himself.
May destruction gnaw mankind! Earth, give
me your roots.

Anyone who wants better from you, give him a
taste of your most powerful poison. What is
this? Gold? Yellow, glittering, precious gold?
No, gods, I didn't make my vow idly.
Give me roots, you pure heavens! This amount
of wealth will make black white; foul fair;
wrong right;
low noble; old young; cowards brave. Ha, you
gods!
Why this? What is this, you gods?
Why, this
will drag your priests and servants away from
you,

Pluck stout men's pillows from below their heads:
This yellow slave
Will knit and break religions, bless the accursed,
Make the hoar leprosy adored, place thieves
And give them title, knee and approbation
With senators on the bench: this is it
That makes the wappen'd widow wed again;
She, whom the spital-house and ulcerous sores
Would cast the gorge at, this embalms and spices
To the April day again. Come, damned earth,
Thou common whore of mankind, that put'st odds
Among the route of nations, I will make thee
Do thy right nature.

March afar off
Ha! a drum ? Thou'rt quick,
But yet I'll bury thee: thou'lt go, strong thief,
When gouty keepers of thee cannot stand.
Nay, stay thou out for earnest.

Keeping some gold

Enter ALCIBIADES, with drum and fife, in warlike manner; PHRYNIA and TIMANDRA

ALCIBIADES
What art thou there? speak.

TIMON
A beast, as thou art. The canker gnaw thy heart,
For showing me again the eyes of man!

ALCIBIADES
What is thy name? Is man so hateful to thee,
That art thyself a man?

TIMON
I am Misanthropos, and hate mankind.
For thy part, I do wish thou wert a dog,
That I might love thee something.

ALCIBIADES
I know thee well;

*and drive strong men to their deaths.
This yellow slave
can make or break religions, bless the cursed,
make the filthy leprosy loved, raise thieves up
and give them titles, respect and equality
with the senators on the bench.
This is the thing
which makes the weary widow marry again:
the one whom hospital patients and ulcerous sores
would vomit just to look at, having this makes her look
in the prime of youth again. Come, damned earth,
you shared whore of mankind, that sets
the nations fighting each other, I will make you*

*do what you always do.
Ha? The drum? You are swift,
but I'll still bury you. You will keep going, you
strong thief, when the gout ridden keepers of
you can no longer stand. No, you stay out here
to be used as a deposit.
[Keeping some gold]*

Who's that there? Speak.

*An animal, the same as you. Make cancer chew
your heart, for making me look at a man again!*

*What is your name? Is mankind so abhorrent to
you, who is a man yourself?*

*I am Misanthrope, and I hate mankind.
As to you, I wish you were a dog,
so I could love you a little.*

I know you well;

But in thy fortunes am unlearn'd and strange.

but I'm unaware of what has happened to you.

TIMON
I know thee too; and more than that I know thee,
I not desire to know. Follow thy drum;
With man's blood paint the ground, gules, gules:
Religious canons, civil laws are cruel;
Then what should war be? This fell whore of thine
Hath in her more destruction than thy sword,
For all her cherubim look.

I know you too; and more than the fact that I know you,
I don't wish to know. Follow your drums;
paint the ground red with the blood of men:
religious rules, civil laws are cruel;
so what should war be? This evil whore of yours
has more powers of destruction than your sword,
for all her sweet looks.

PHRYNIA
Thy lips rot off!

May your lips rot and fall off!

TIMON
I will not kiss thee; then the rot returns
To thine own lips again.

I won't kiss you; that way the rot stays
on your own lips where it belongs.

ALCIBIADES
How came the noble Timon to this change?

What happened to make the noble Timon change like this?

TIMON
As the moon does, by wanting light to give:
But then renew I could not, like the moon;
There were no suns to borrow of.

In the same way as happens to the moon, when he has no light to give:
but then I couldn't be renewed, like the moon;
there were no suns to borrow from.

ALCIBIADES
Noble Timon,
What friendship may I do thee?

Noble Timon,
is there anything I can do for you?

TIMON
None, but to
Maintain my opinion.

Nothing, except help me
keep my opinion of mankind.

ALCIBIADES
What is it, Timon?

How will I do that, Timon?

TIMON
Promise me friendship, but perform none: if thou
wilt not promise, the gods plague thee, for thou art
a man! if thou dost perform, confound thee, for

Promise me friendship, but don't do anything about it: if you
won't promise, may the gods attack you, for being
a man! If you do keep your promise, you'll still

thou art a man!

ALCIBIADES
I have heard in some sort of thy miseries.

TIMON
Thou saw'st them, when I had prosperity.

ALCIBIADES
I see them now; then was a blessed time.

TIMON
As thine is now, held with a brace of harlots.

TIMANDRA
Is this the Athenian minion, whom the world
Voiced so regardfully?

TIMON
Art thou Timandra?

TIMANDRA
Yes.

TIMON
Be a whore still: they love thee not that use
thee;
Give them diseases, leaving with thee their lust.
Make use of thy salt hours: season the slaves
For tubs and baths; bring down rose-cheeked
youth
To the tub-fast and the diet.

TIMANDRA
Hang thee, monster!

ALCIBIADES
Pardon him, sweet Timandra; for his wits
Are drown'd and lost in his calamities.
I have but little gold of late, brave Timon,
The want whereof doth daily make revolt
In my penurious band: I have heard, and
grieved,
How cursed Athens, mindless of thy worth,
Forgetting thy great deeds, when neighbour
states,

be damned, because you are a man!

I have heard something about your misfortunes.

You saw them, when I was rich.

*I can see them now; you were blessed back
then.*

As you are now, tied up with a pair of tarts.

*Is this the favourite of Athens, whom everyone
used to speak so well of?*

Are you Timandra?

Yes.

*Carry on being a whore: those who use you do
not love you;
take their lust away and give them diseases.
Make use of the time that you're in season: get
the slaves ready for the cure for the clap;
reduced the rosy cheeked youth
to the sweating baths and the curing diet.*

Hang you, monster!

*Excuse him, sweet Timandra; his wits
have been drowned and lost in his misfortunes.
I haven't much money at the moment, brave
Timon, the lack of which causes mutiny daily
in my poverty stricken band: I have heard, and
been sorry for,
the way cursed Athens, disregarding your
worth, forgetting your great deeds, when
neighbouring states*

But for thy sword and fortune, trod upon them,--

would have trodden on them without your swords and wealth--

TIMON
I prithee, beat thy drum, and get thee gone.

Please, beat your drum and go.

ALCIBIADES
I am thy friend, and pity thee, dear Timon.

I am your friend, and pity you, dear Timon.

TIMON
How dost thou pity him whom thou dost trouble?
I had rather be alone.

If you pity someone why are you bothering him?
I would rather be alone.

ALCIBIADES
Why, fare thee well:
Here is some gold for thee.

Well, farewell then:
here is some gold for you.

TIMON
Keep it, I cannot eat it.

Keep it, I can't eat it.

ALCIBIADES
When I have laid proud Athens on a heap,--

When I have beaten proud Athens to the ground--

TIMON
Warr'st thou 'gainst Athens?

Are you going to war against Athens?

ALCIBIADES
Ay, Timon, and have cause.

Yes, Timon, and I have good reason.

TIMON
The gods confound them all in thy conquest;
And thee after, when thou hast conquer'd!

May the gods defeat them all in your conquest;
and you after that, when you have won!

ALCIBIADES
Why me, Timon?

Why me, Timon?

TIMON
That, by killing of villains,
Thou wast born to conquer my country.
Put up thy gold: go on,--here's gold,--go on;
Be as a planetary plague, when Jove
Will o'er some high-viced city hang his poison
In the sick air: let not thy sword skip one:
Pity not honour'd age for his white beard;
He is an usurer: strike me the counterfeit

Because by killing villains
you shall conquer my country.
Put away your gold. Go on. Here's some gold.
Go on. Be like a plague from the heavens, when
Jove blows his poison through the sick air of
some immoral city. Don't let your sword miss a
single person. Don't pity the old man for his
white beard: he's a moneylender. Cut down the

matron;
It is her habit only that is honest,
Herself's a bawd: let not the virgin's cheek
Make soft thy trenchant sword; for those milk-
paps,
That through the window-bars bore at men's
eyes,
Are not within the leaf of pity writ,
But set them down horrible traitors: spare not
the babe,
Whose dimpled smiles from fools exhaust their
mercy;
Think it a bastard, whom the oracle
Hath doubtfully pronounced thy throat shall
cut,
And mince it sans remorse: swear against
objects;
Put armour on thine ears and on thine eyes;
Whose proof, nor yells of mothers, maids, nor
babes,
Nor sight of priests in holy vestments bleeding,
Shall pierce a jot. There's gold to pay soldiers:
Make large confusion; and, thy fury spent,
Confounded be thyself! Speak not, be gone.

fake lady for me:
it's only her clothes which are respectable,
she is a tart. Don't let the virgin's looks
hold back your sword: those white breasts,
which peep through their dresses to catch men's
eyes,
not included on the list of things to be spared,
they are written down as horrible traitors.
Don't spare the baby
whose sweet smile gains mercy from false:
think of it as a bastard, whom the Oracle
has terrifyingly predicted will cut your throat,
and chop it up without pity. Don't let any
protests put you off.
Cover up your ears and your eyes with armour
through whose strength the yells of mothers,
maids or babies,
nor the sight of priests bleeding in their holy
robes
cannot pierce. Here's gold to pay your soldiers.
Cause great chaos; and, when your anger is
spent,
be damned to you! Don't speak, go.

ALCIBIADES
Hast thou gold yet? I'll take the gold thou
givest me,
Not all thy counsel.

Do you still have gold? I'll take the gold you
give me,
not your advice.

TIMON
Dost thou, or dost thou not, heaven's curse
upon thee!

May heaven curse you, whether you do or not!

PHRYNIA TIMANDRA
Give us some gold, good Timon: hast thou
more?

Give us some gold, good Timon: do you have
more?

TIMON
Enough to make a whore forswear her trade,
And to make whores, a bawd. Hold up, you
sluts,
Your aprons mountant: you are not oathable,
Although, I know, you 'll swear, terribly swear
Into strong shudders and to heavenly agues
The immortal gods that hear you,--spare your

Enough to make a whore give up her business,
to turn whores into brothel keepers. You sluts,
hold out your aprons. You can't be made to
swear oaths,
although I know you'll swear, swear terribly
so that the awful gods that listen to you will be
sent into fits and trembling. Don't bother with

oaths,
I'll trust to your conditions: be whores still;
And he whose pious breath seeks to convert you,
Be strong in whore, allure him, burn him up;
Let your close fire predominate his smoke,
And be no turncoats: yet may your pains, six months,
Be quite contrary: and thatch your poor thin roofs
With burthens of the dead;--some that were hang'd,
No matter:--wear them, betray with them: whore still;
Paint till a horse may mire upon your face,
A pox of wrinkles!

PHRYNIA TIMANDRA
Well, more gold: what then?
Believe't, that we'll do any thing for gold.

TIMON
Consumptions sow
In hollow bones of man; strike their sharp shins,
And mar men's spurring. Crack the lawyer's voice,
That he may never more false title plead,
Nor sound his quillets shrilly: hoar the flamen,
That scolds against the quality of flesh,
And not believes himself: down with the nose,
Down with it flat; take the bridge quite away
Of him that, his particular to foresee,
Smells from the general weal: make curl'd-pate ruffians bald;
And let the unscarr'd braggarts of the war
Derive some pain from you: plague all;
That your activity may defeat and quell
The source of all erection. There's more gold:
Do you damn others, and let this damn you,
And ditches grave you all!

PHRYNIA TIMANDRA
More counsel with more money, bounteous Timon.

oaths:
I'll trust your nature. Remain as whores;
and when someone tries to convert you with pious words,
be a strong whore, draw him in, burn him up;
let your burning passions triumph over his piety,
and don't be traitors; but I hope you also suffer for the next six months. And cover
your poor thin hair with wigs made from the hair of the dead—
some of them were hanged, it doesn't matter;
wear them and use them for betrayal: remain a whore;
put on so much paint that a horse could sink in it: be damned to wrinkles!

Good, more gold: what then?
You can be sure that we will do anything for gold.

Sow consumption
into the hollow bones of man; rot their legs
to spoil their riding. Ruin the lawyer's throat,
so he can never act for the fraudster again,
or make his quibbling arguments: give the clap
to the priest who speaks against the weaknesses of the flesh
and doesn't follow his own teaching: rot away his nose,
make it flat; remove the bridge completely of the one who, in order to look after himself,
steals from the public. Make curly haired ruffians bald,
and let the unscarred boasting soldier
get a wound from you: give the clap to them all,
so that your activity can subdue
all lust. There's more gold.
You damn others, and let this damn you,
and may you all die in the ditch!

Give us more advice and more money, generous Timon.

TIMON
More whore, more mischief first; I have given
you earnest.

I want to see you causing more whorish
mischief first; I have paid your fee.

ALCIBIADES
Strike up the drum towards Athens! Farewell,
Timon:
If I thrive well, I'll visit thee again.

Strike up the drum for the march on Athens!
Farewell, Timon:
if I succeed, I'll visit you again.

TIMON
If I hope well, I'll never see thee more.

If I get my wish, I'll never see you again.

ALCIBIADES
I never did thee harm.

I never did you any harm.

TIMON
Yes, thou spokest well of me.

You did, you spoke well of me.

ALCIBIADES
Call'st thou that harm?

Do you call that doing harm?

TIMON
Men daily find it. Get thee away, and take
Thy beagles with thee.

Men find it is every day. Off you go, and take
your dogs with you.

ALCIBIADES
We but offend him. Strike!

We're just upsetting him. Strike up the march!

Drum beats. Exeunt ALCIBIADES, PHRYNIA, and TIMANDRA

TIMON
That nature, being sick of man's unkindness,
Should yet be hungry! Common mother, thou,

It's amazing that people who have had an
overdose of man's unkindness
still want more! Universal mother, you
[digging]

Digging
Whose womb unmeasurable, and infinite
breast,
Teems, and feeds all; whose self-same mettle,
Whereof thy proud child, arrogant man, is
puff'd,
Engenders the black toad and adder blue,
The gilded newt and eyeless venom'd worm,
With all the abhorred births below crisp heaven
Whereon Hyperion's quickening fire doth shine;
Yield him, who all thy human sons doth hate,

whose infinite womb and breast
breeds and feeds everything; the same essence
which makes your proud child, arrogant man,
also makes the black toad and the blue adder,
the golden newt and blind poisonous worm,
and all the other revolting births below the
pure sky where the sun shines;
give the person whom all your human sons hate
just one poor root from your bounty!
Seal up your fertile and prolific womb,
don't give birth to any more ungrateful men!

From forth thy plenteous bosom, one poor root!
Ensear thy fertile and conceptious womb,
Let it no more bring out ingrateful man!
Go great with tigers, dragons, wolves, and bears;
Teem with new monsters, whom thy upward face
Hath to the marbled mansion all above
Never presented!--O, a root,--dear thanks!--
Dry up thy marrows, vines, and plough-torn leas;
Whereof ungrateful man, with liquorish draughts
And morsels unctuous, greases his pure mind,
That from it all consideration slips!

Enter APEMANTUS
More man? plague, plague!

APEMANTUS
I was directed hither: men report
Thou dost affect my manners, and dost use them.

TIMON
'Tis, then, because thou dost not keep a dog,
Whom I would imitate: consumption catch thee!

APEMANTUS
This is in thee a nature but affected;
A poor unmanly melancholy sprung
From change of fortune. Why this spade? this place?
This slave-like habit? and these looks of care?
Thy flatterers yet wear silk, drink wine, lie soft;
Hug their diseased perfumes, and have forgot
That ever Timon was. Shame not these woods,
By putting on the cunning of a carper.
Be thou a flatterer now, and seek to thrive
By that which has undone thee: hinge thy knee,
And let his very breath, whom thou'lt observe,
Blow off thy cap; praise his most vicious strain,
And call it excellent: thou wast told thus;
Thou gavest thine ears like tapsters that bid welcome

Become pregnant with tigers, dragons, wolves and bears;
swell with new monsters, which have never before been seen on the face of the earth!
Oh, a root!–Much thanks!–
Dry up all vegetables, vines and ploughed fields,
which ungrateful man uses to make liquor and greasy food, which makes his pure mind so greasy
that all ability to think slips from it!

More humanity? A plague on it!

I was told to come here. Men are saying that you are copying me.

If I am it's only because you haven't got a dog I could imitate instead: may consumption overwhelm you!

This is just an affectation on your part;
a poor unmanly depression coming from your change of fortunes. Why this spade? This place?
These slave's clothes? And these careworn looks? Your flatterers are still wearing silk, drinking wine, sleeping in soft beds;
they are cuddling their diseased mistresses, and have forgotten that Timon ever existed. Don't embarrass these woods by taking up the profession of a cynic. Become a flatterer yourself, and try to succeed through the thing which caused your downfall: bend the knee, bow down so low that the person you're flattering can blow off your cap with his breath; praise his most revolting quality,

To knaves and all approachers: 'tis most just
That thou turn rascal; hadst thou wealth again,
Rascals should have 't. Do not assume my
likeness.

and call it excellent: this is what others did to you; you were like a barman who is prepared to listen to any knave who comes in: it would be very apt for you to become a rascal; if you had wealth again, rascals would have it. Don't copy me.

TIMON
Were I like thee, I'ld throw away myself.

If I was like you, I'd kill myself.

APEMANTUS
Thou hast cast away thyself, being like thyself;
A madman so long, now a fool. What, think'st
That the bleak air, thy boisterous chamberlain,
Will put thy shirt on warm? will these moss'd
trees,
That have outlived the eagle, page thy heels,
And skip where thou point'st out? will the
cold brook,
Candied with ice, caudle thy morning taste,
To cure thy o'er-night's surfeit? Call the
creatures
Whose naked natures live in an the spite
Of wreakful heaven, whose bare unhoused
trunks,
To the conflicting elements exposed,
Answer mere nature; bid them flatter thee;
O, thou shalt find--

You've already killed yourself, by being who you are; you were a madman so long, now you're a fool. What, do you think that the cold air, your hearty servant, will give you a nice warm shirt? Will these moss covered trees, that have lived longer than the eagles, follow you around and do whatever you tell them? Will the cold stream, covered with ice, bring you a warm drink in the morning to soothe the results of your indulgence? Call the creatures who live out here exposed to all the spite of vengeful heaven, whose bare roofless bodies are exposed to all the elements, enduring nature in its undiluted form; tell them to flatter you. Oh, you shall find—

TIMON
A fool of thee: depart.

You're a fool: go.

APEMANTUS
I love thee better now than e'er I did.

I like you better now than I ever did.

TIMON
I hate thee worse.

I hate you more.

APEMANTUS
Why?

Why?

TIMON
Thou flatter'st misery.

You flatter misery.

APEMANTUS
I flatter not; but say thou art a caitiff.

I don't flatter; but I say you are a wretch.

TIMON

Why dost thou seek me out?

Why did you look for me?

APEMANTUS

To vex thee.

To annoy you.

TIMON

Always a villain's office or a fool's.
Dost please thyself in't?

The job of a villain or a fool.
Do you enjoy it?

APEMANTUS

Ay.

Yes.

TIMON

What! a knave too?

What! You're a knave as well?

APEMANTUS

If thou didst put this sour-cold habit on
To castigate thy pride, 'twere well: but thou
Dost it enforcedly; thou'ldst courtier be again,
Wert thou not beggar. Willing misery
Outlives encertain pomp, is crown'd before:
The one is filling still, never complete;
The other, at high wish: best state, contentless,
Hath a distracted and most wretched being,
Worse than the worst, content.
Thou shouldst desire to die, being miserable.

If you assumed this sour cold dress to
punish your pride, that would be good: but you
do it from necessity; you would be a courtier
again, if you weren't a beggar. Gladly accepted
misery is better than uncertain wealth, the gods
prefer it; one is always trying to get more,
never satisfied, the other is as complete as you
could wish: the man in the best position without
happiness is completely wretched, much worse
than someone in a terrible position who is
happy. You should want to die, as you're
miserable.

TIMON

Not by his breath that is more miserable.
Thou art a slave, whom Fortune's tender arm
With favour never clasp'd; but bred a dog.
Hadst thou, like us from our first swath, proceeded
The sweet degrees that this brief world affords
To such as may the passive drugs of it
Freely command, thou wouldst have plunged thyself
In general riot; melted down thy youth
In different beds of lust; and never learn'd
The icy precepts of respect, but follow'd
The sugar'd game before thee. But myself,
Who had the world as my confectionary,
The mouths, the tongues, the eyes and hearts of men

Not on the advice of someone who is more
miserable. You are a slave, whom fortune has
never embraced; she made you a dog.
Had you been from birth, like me, given
all the sweet things that this short life allows
to those who have access to its
sweet things, you would have thrown yourself
in with gusto; you would have wasted your
youth
in various lustful beds; you would never have
learned
to see everything in proportion, but enjoyed
all the sweetness offered to you. But I,
for whom the whole world was a sweet shop,
had the mouths, tongues, eyes and hearts of
men

At duty, more than I could frame employment,
That numberless upon me stuck as leaves
Do on the oak, hive with one winter's brush
Fell from their boughs and left me open, bare
For every storm that blows: I, to bear this,
That never knew but better, is some burden:
Thy nature did commence in sufferance, time
Hath made thee hard in't. Why shouldst thou
hate men?
They never flatter'd thee: what hast thou given?
If thou wilt curse, thy father, that poor rag,
Must be thy subject, who in spite put stuff
To some she beggar and compounded thee
Poor rogue hereditary. Hence, be gone!
If thou hadst not been born the worst of men,
Thou hadst been a knave and flatterer.

APEMANTUS
Art thou proud yet?

TIMON
Ay, that I am not thee.

APEMANTUS
I, that I was
No prodigal.

TIMON
I, that I am one now:
Were all the wealth I have shut up in thee,
I'ld give thee leave to hang it. Get thee gone.
That the whole life of Athens were in this!
Thus would I eat it.

Eating a root

APEMANTUS
Here; I will mend thy feast.

Offering him a root

TIMON
First mend my company, take away thyself.

APEMANTUS
So I shall mend mine own, by the lack of thine.

at my service, more than I could find work for,
an infinite number covering me like leaves
on an oak tree; at the first touch of winter
they fell from their branches and left me
exposed to every storm that blows: for me to
bear this, having only known better days, is a
great burden: your life began with suffering,
time has hardened you to it. Why should you
hate men?
They never flattered you: what have you given?
If you want to apportion blame your poor rag
of a father must be your subject, who out of
spite impregnated
some female beggar and made you,
a poor rogue by birth. Get out of here!
If you hadn't been born in the lowest situation
you would have been a knave and a flatterer.

Are you still proud?

Yes, that I am not you.

I'm proud that I didn't
throw money around.

I'm proud I did:
if all the wealth I have was in your body,
I'd give you permission to hang yourself. Go
away. I wish all the lives in Athens were in this
root! I would eat it like this.

Here; I will improve your feast.

First improve my company, by going away.

That way I would improve my own, by not

TIMON
'Tis not well mended so, it is but botch'd;
if not, I would it were.

APEMANTUS
What wouldst thou have to Athens?

TIMON
Thee thither in a whirlwind. If thou wilt,
Tell them there I have gold; look, so I have.

APEMANTUS
Here is no use for gold.

TIMON
The best and truest;
For here it sleeps, and does no hired harm.

APEMANTUS
Where liest o' nights, Timon?

TIMON
Under that's above me.
Where feed'st thou o' days, Apemantus?

APEMANTUS
Where my stomach finds meat; or, rather,
where I eat
it.

TIMON
Would poison were obedient and knew my
mind!

APEMANTUS
Where wouldst thou send it?

TIMON
To sauce thy dishes.

APEMANTUS
The middle of humanity thou never knewest,
but the
extremity of both ends: when thou wast in thy
gilt

having yours.

*That wouldn't mend it, just botch it up;
whatever the case, I wish you would do it.*

What would you like to give to Athens?

*You, in the middle of a whirlwind. If you want,
tell the people there that I have gold; look, I
have.*

Gold is useless here.

*It has its best and truest use here;
it sleeps here, and can't buy any evil.*

Where do you sleep at night, Timon?

*Out in the open air.
Where do you eat in the day, Apemantus?*

*Wherever my stomach finds food; or, rather,
where I eat
it.*

I wish I had control of poison!

Where would you send it?

To spice up your food.

*You never knew the middle road of humanity,
just the
highest and lowest: when you had all your fine
clothes*

and thy perfume, they mocked thee for too much
curiosity; in thy rags thou knowest none, but art despised for the contrary. There's a medlar for thee, eat it.

TIMON
On what I hate I feed not.

APEMANTUS
Dost hate a medlar?

TIMON
Ay, though it look like thee.

APEMANTUS
An thou hadst hated meddlers sooner, thou shouldst
have loved thyself better now. What man didst thou
ever know unthrift that was beloved after his means?

TIMON
Who, without those means thou talkest of, didst thou
ever know beloved?

APEMANTUS
Myself.

TIMON
I understand thee; thou hadst some means to keep a
dog.

APEMANTUS
What things in the world canst thou nearest compare
to thy flatterers?

TIMON
Women nearest; but men, men are the things themselves. What wouldst thou do with the world,
Apemantus, if it lay in thy power?

and your perfume, you were mocked for being too
delicate; in your rags you have no delicacy, and are despised for it. There's a medlar for you, eat it.

I don't eat what I hate.

You hate a medlar?

Yes, though it looks like you.

If you had hated meddlers earlier, you would love yourself better now. Did you ever know a profligate man who was loved once his money was gone?

Did you ever know anyone who was loved who didn't
have the money that you talk about?

Me.

I understand you; you had just enough money to keep a
dog.

What is there in the world that you can most closely
compare to your flatterers?

Women are closest; but men, men are all complete
flatterers. What would you do with the world, Apemantus, if you had the power?

APEMANTUS

Give it the beasts, to be rid of the men.

I'd give it to the animals, to get rid of men.

TIMON

Wouldst thou have thyself fall in the confusion of
men, and remain a beast with the beasts?

Would you like to be part of the fall of man, and remain an animal with the other animals?

APEMANTUS

Ay, Timon.

Yes, Timon.

TIMON

A beastly ambition, which the gods grant thee t'
attain to! If thou wert the lion, the fox would
beguile thee; if thou wert the lamb, the fox would
eat thee: if thou wert the fox, the lion would
suspect thee, when peradventure thou wert
accused by
the ass: if thou wert the ass, thy dulness would
torment thee, and still thou livedst but as a
breakfast to the wolf: if thou wert the wolf, thy
greediness would afflict thee, and oft thou shouldst
hazard thy life for thy dinner: wert thou the
unicorn, pride and wrath would confound thee and
make thine own self the conquest of thy fury: wert
thou a bear, thou wouldst be killed by the horse:
wert thou a horse, thou wouldst be seized by the
leopard: wert thou a leopard, thou wert german to
the lion and the spots of thy kindred were jurors on
thy life: all thy safety were remotion and thy
defence absence. What beast couldst thou be, that
were not subject to a beast? and what a beast art
thou already, that seest not thy loss in
transformation!

A horrible desire, may the gods grant it to you! If you were a lion, you would be tricked by a fox; if you were a lamb, the fox would eat you; if you were a fox, the lion would suspect you, if you happen to be accused by the ass; if you were an ass, your stupidity would torment you, and all you would be living for would be to make a breakfast for the wolf; if you were a wolf, your greediness would torture you, and you would often risk your life for your dinner; if you were a unicorn, pride and anger would confuse you and you would cause your own downfall in your anger; if you were a bear, you would be killed by a horse; if you were a horse, you would be taken by a leopard; if you were a leopard, you would be related to the lion and you would be punished for his transgressions; the only way you could be safe would be to run away, being absent would be your defence. What animal could you be, that didn't suffer at the hands of another animal? And what an animal you are already, if you can't see that you would be worse off as an animal!

APEMANTUS

If thou couldst please me with speaking to me,

If anything you said could please me, you

thou
mightst have hit upon it here: the commonwealth of
Athens is become a forest of beasts.

might have just said it: the state of
Athens has become a forest of animals.

TIMON
How has the ass broke the wall, that thou art
out of the city?

How did the ass break through the wall, to let
you out of the city?

APEMANTUS
Yonder comes a poet and a painter: the plague of
company light upon thee! I will fear to catch it
and give way: when I know not what else to do, I'll
see thee again.

Here comes a poet and painter: may the plague of
society land on you! I don't want to catch it
so I'll go: when I can't think of anything else to do, I'll
come back and see you.

TIMON
When there is nothing living but thee, thou shalt be
welcome. I had rather be a beggar's dog than
Apemantus.

When you are the last living creature, you will be
welcome. I would rather be a beggar's dog than
Apemantus.

APEMANTUS
Thou art the cap of all the fools alive.

You are the King of fools.

TIMON
Would thou wert clean enough to spit upon!

I wish you were clean enough to spit on!

APEMANTUS
A plague on thee! thou art too bad to curse.

A plague on you! You are too wicked for simple
curses.

TIMON
All villains that do stand by thee are pure.

Any villain standing next to you would look
pure in comparison.

APEMANTUS
There is no leprosy but what thou speak'st.

There is no leprosy to compare with what you
say.

TIMON
If I name thee.
I'll beat thee, but I should infect my hands.

If I say your name.
I would beat you, but I don't want to catch
anything.

APEMANTUS
I would my tongue could rot them off!

I wish my tongue could rot your hands off!

TIMON

Away, thou issue of a mangy dog!
Choler does kill me that thou art alive;
I swound to see thee.

APEMANTUS
Would thou wouldst burst!

TIMON
Away,
Thou tedious rogue! I am sorry I shall lose
A stone by thee.

Throws a stone at him

APEMANTUS
Beast!

TIMON
Slave!

APEMANTUS
Toad!

TIMON
Rogue, rogue, rogue!
I am sick of this false world, and will love
nought
But even the mere necessities upon 't.
Then, Timon, presently prepare thy grave;
Lie where the light foam the sea may beat
Thy grave-stone daily: make thine epitaph,
That death in me at others' lives may laugh.

To the gold
O thou sweet king-killer, and dear divorce
'Twixt natural son and sire! thou bright defiler
Of Hymen's purest bed! thou valiant Mars!
Thou ever young, fresh, loved and delicate
wooer,
Whose blush doth thaw the consecrated snow
That lies on Dian's lap! thou visible god,
That solder'st close impossibilities,
And makest them kiss! that speak'st with
every tongue,
To every purpose! O thou touch of hearts!
Think, thy slave man rebels, and by thy virtue

Get lost, you son of a bitch!
It tortures me to see that you are alive;
it makes me faint to see you.

I wish you would burst!

Get lost,
you tedious scoundrel! I am sorry to have to
waste a stone on you.

Animal!

Slave!

Toad!

Rogue, rogue, rogue!
I am sick of this false world, and will love
nothing
except the necessities of life.
So, Timon, go and dig your own grave at once;
put it where the light foam of the sea can wash
against your gravestone daily: make your
epitaph that through me death is laughing at
the lives of others.
[To the gold]
Oh you sweet killer of kings, that causes
division between fathers and their natural sons!
You bright polluter
of the pure wedding bed, you brave adulterer,
you always young, fresh, loved and delicate
suitor, whose blush could thaw the holy snow
that lies in Diana's lap! You material god,
that brings incompatible things together,
and makes them kiss! You govern all speech
and all purposes! Oh you ruler of hearts!
You can see your slave, man, is rebelling, you
have

Set them into confounding odds, that beasts
May have the world in empire!

*set all men against each other, so beasts
will rule the world!*

APEMANTUS
Would 'twere so!
But not till I am dead. I'll say thou'st gold:
Thou wilt be throng'd to shortly.

*I wish it would happen!
But not in my lifetime. I'll say you have gold:
you will be mobbed shortly.*

TIMON
Throng'd to!

Mobbed!

APEMANTUS
Ay.

Yes.

TIMON
Thy back, I prithee.

Let me see you going, please.

APEMANTUS
Live, and love thy misery.

Live, and enjoy your misery.

TIMON
Long live so, and so die.   I am quit.

*Live a long miserable life, and then die. I'm
finished.*

Exit APEMANTUS

Moe things like men! Eat, Timon, and abhor
them.

More men coming! Eat, Timon, and shun them.

Enter Banditti

First Bandit
Where should he have this gold? It is some
poor
fragment, some slender sort of his remainder:
the
mere want of gold, and the falling-from of his
friends, drove him into this melancholy.

*Where would he have got this gold from? It'll
just be
some tiny bit left over from his fortune: it was
a lack of gold, and his friends abandoning
him, which drove him into this depression.*

Second Bandit
It is noised he hath a mass of treasure.

It's rumoured he has a great treasure.

Third Bandit
Let us make the assay upon him: if he care not
for't, he will supply us easily; if he covetously
reserve it, how shall's get it?

*Let's put him to the test: if he doesn't care
about it, he'll gladly give it to us; if he greedily
hoards it, how shall we get it?*

Second Bandit
True; for he bears it not about him, 'tis hid.

That's true, for he is not carrying it with him, it's hidden.

First Bandit
Is not this he?

Isn't this him?

Banditti
Where?

Where?

Second Bandit
'Tis his description.

He looks like his description.

Third Bandit
He; I know him.

It's him; I recognise him.

Banditti
Save thee, Timon.

God save you, Timon.

TIMON
Now, thieves?

What's this, thieves?

Banditti
Soldiers, not thieves.

Soldiers, not thieves.

TIMON
Both too; and women's sons.

You are both; and sons of women.

Banditti
We are not thieves, but men that much do want.

We are not thieves, but very much in need.

TIMON
Your greatest want is, you want much of meat.
Why should you want? Behold, the earth hath roots;
Within this mile break forth a hundred springs;
The oaks bear mast, the briers scarlet hips;
The bounteous housewife, nature, on each bush
Lays her full mess before you. Want! why want?

Your greatest need is, you want plenty of meat. Why do you need it? Look, the Earth has roots; there are a hundred streams within a mile of here;
the oaks have acorns, the brambles red fruit; the generous housewife of nature has laid out her great feast in front of you. Need! Why do you need?

First Bandit
We cannot live on grass, on berries, water,
As beasts and birds and fishes.

We can't live on grass, berries and water, like animals and birds and fish.

TIMON
Nor on the beasts themselves, the birds, and

You can't live on the animals themselves, the

fishes;
You must eat men. Yet thanks I must you con
That you are thieves profess'd, that you work not
In holier shapes: for there is boundless theft
In limited professions. Rascal thieves,
Here's gold. Go, suck the subtle blood o' the grape,
Till the high fever seethe your blood to froth,
And so 'scape hanging: trust not the physician;
His antidotes are poison, and he slays
Moe than you rob: take wealth and lives together.
Do villany, do, since you protest to do't,
Like workmen. I'll example you with thievery.
The sun's a thief, and with his great attraction
Robs the vast sea: the moon's an arrant thief,
And her pale fire she snatches from the sun:
The sea's a thief, whose liquid surge resolves
The moon into salt tears: the earth's a thief,
That feeds and breeds by a composture stolen
From general excrement: each thing's a thief:
The laws, your curb and whip, in their rough power
Have uncheque'd theft. Love not yourselves: away,
Rob one another. There's more gold. Cut throats:
All that you meet are thieves: to Athens go,
Break open shops; nothing can you steal,
But thieves do lose it: steal no less for this
I give you; and gold confound you howsoe'er!
Amen.

Third Bandit
Has almost charmed me from my profession, by
persuading me to it.

First Bandit
'Tis in the malice of mankind that he thus advises
us; not to have us thrive in our mystery.

Second Bandit
I'll believe him as an enemy, and give over my

birds and fish;
you have to eat men. But I must thank you for
admitting that you are thieves, that you don't pretend
to be something better: for there is limitless
thievery in business. Rascally thieves,
take this gold. Go, guzzle wine
until your blood starts to boil,
and so escape hanging. Don't trust the doctor;
his medicines are poison, and he kills
more people than you rob: he takes their money
and their lives together.
Since villainy is your profession then do it
professionally. I'll justify your thievery for you;
the sun is a thief, with his great pull
he robs the vast sea: the moon is definitely a thief,
she steals her pale light from the Sun:
the sea is a thief, stealing the power of the
moon for its tides: the Earth is a thief,
feeding and breeding with a fertiliser stolen
from dung: everything is a thief:
the law, which constrains and whips you, has the power
for unrestrained theft. Don't respect yourselves: go,
and rob each other. Here's some more gold.
Cut some throats: everyone you meet is a thief:
go to Athens, break open the shops; there's
nothing you can steal, that you're not stealing
from thieves: don't steal less just because you
have what I've given you; and may
gold lead you to damnation! Amen.

He's almost dissuaded me from thievery, by
encouraging me to do it.

He's talking to us like this out of hatred for mankind,
not because he wants us to do well in our profession.

I'll do the opposite of what my enemy says, and

trade.

First Bandit
Let us first see peace in Athens: there is no time
so miserable but a man may be true.

Exeunt Banditti

Enter FLAVIUS

FLAVIUS
O you gods!
Is yond despised and ruinous man my lord?
Full of decay and failing? O monument
And wonder of good deeds evilly bestow'd!
What an alteration of honour
Has desperate want made!
What viler thing upon the earth than friends
Who can bring noblest minds to basest ends!
How rarely does it meet with this time's guise,
When man was wish'd to love his enemies!
Grant I may ever love, and rather woo
Those that would mischief me than those that
do!
Has caught me in his eye: I will present
My honest grief unto him; and, as my lord,
Still serve him with my life. My dearest master!

TIMON
Away! what art thou?

FLAVIUS
Have you forgot me, sir?

TIMON
Why dost ask that? I have forgot all men;
Then, if thou grant'st thou'rt a man, I have
forgot thee.

FLAVIUS
An honest poor servant of yours.

TIMON
Then I know thee not:
I never had honest man about me, I; all
I kept were knaves, to serve in meat to villains.

give up my profession.

*Let's wait until there is peace in Athens: we
don't have to hurry about reforming when there
are better things to do.*

*Oh you gods!
Is that despicable and ruined man my lord?
Full of decay and weakness? What an example
of good deeds done for the wrong people!
What a great change
desperate poverty has made!
What is there on earth more horrible than
friends who reduce the noblest minds to such a
position! How admirably it fits with the way of
the world, that a man's enemies are the ones he
loved! If I ever love let me love those
who want to harm me, rather than those who
say they love me!
He has seen me: I will tell him
how sad I am; and, as he is my lord,
I will carry on serving him with my life. My
dearest master!*

Go away! Who are you?

Have you forgotten me, sir?

*Why are you asking that? I have forgotten all
men; so, if you say you are a man, I have
forgotten you.*

I am an honest poor servant of yours.

*Then I don't know you: I never had an honest
man with me; all my servants were knaves, used
to bring in food for villains.*

FLAVIUS

The gods are witness,
Ne'er did poor steward wear a truer grief
For his undone lord than mine eyes for you.

*The gods are witnesses to the fact
that no poor steward was ever so sad
for his fallen master than I am for you.*

TIMON

What, dost thou weep? Come nearer. Then I
love thee,
Because thou art a woman, and disclaim'st
Flinty mankind; whose eyes do never give
But thorough lust and laughter. Pity's sleeping:
Strange times, that weep with laughing, not
with weeping!

*What, are you weeping? Come closer. Then I
love you,
because you are a woman, and aren't part of
stony hearted mankind; their eyes never shed
tears except through lust and laughter. Pity is
sleeping: these are strange times, that weep
with laughter, not with sorrow!*

FLAVIUS

I beg of you to know me, good my lord,
To accept my grief and whilst this poor wealth
lasts
To entertain me as your steward still.

*I beg you to recognise me, my good lord,
to accept my sorrow and let me be your steward
for as long as this poor wealth lasts.*

TIMON

Had I a steward
So true, so just, and now so comfortable?
It almost turns my dangerous nature mild.
Let me behold thy face. Surely, this man
Was born of woman.
Forgive my general and exceptless rashness,
You perpetual-sober gods! I do proclaim
One honest man--mistake me not--but one;
No more, I pray,--and he's a steward.
How fain would I have hated all mankind!
And thou redeem'st thyself: but all, save thee,
I fell with curses.
Methinks thou art more honest now than wise;
For, by oppressing and betraying me,
Thou mightst have sooner got another service:
For many so arrive at second masters,
Upon their first lord's neck. But tell me true--
For I must ever doubt, though ne'er so sure--
Is not thy kindness subtle, covetous,
If not a usuring kindness, and, as rich men deal
gifts,
Expecting in return twenty for one?

*Did I have a steward
who was so true, so just, and is now so
comforting? This almost calms my anger.
Let me see your face. Surely, this is a man
born of a woman.
Forgive my indiscriminate anger,
you always sensible gods! I announce that there
is one honest man–don't misunderstand me–
there's only one; no more, I hope–and he's a
steward. How much I wanted to hate all
mankind! You have redeemed yourself, but I
strike all the rest with curses.
I think you've got more honesty than sense now;
for, by oppressing and betraying me,
you might soon have got another job:
so many get service with their second masters
by betraying their first lords. But tell me
truthfully– for I must always doubt, however
sure I am– isn't your kindness cunning, greedy,
the kindness of a moneylender, given as rich
men give gifts,
expecting twenty in return for one?*

FLAVIUS

No, my most worthy master; in whose breast

No, my most worthy master; in whose heart

110

Doubt and suspect, alas, are placed too late:
You should have fear'd false times when you did feast:
Suspect still comes where an estate is least.
That which I show, heaven knows, is merely love,
Duty and zeal to your unmatched mind,
Care of your food and living; and, believe it,
My most honour'd lord,
For any benefit that points to me,
Either in hope or present, I'ld exchange
For this one wish, that you had power and wealth
To requite me, by making rich yourself.

TIMON
Look thee, 'tis so! Thou singly honest man,
Here, take: the gods out of my misery
Have sent thee treasure. Go, live rich and happy;
But thus condition'd: thou shalt build from men;
Hate all, curse all, show charity to none,
But let the famish'd flesh slide from the bone,
Ere thou relieve the beggar; give to dogs
What thou deny'st to men; let prisons swallow 'em,
Debts wither 'em to nothing; be men like blasted woods,
And may diseases lick up their false bloods!
And so farewell and thrive.

FLAVIUS
O, let me stay,
And comfort you, my master.

TIMON
If thou hatest curses,
Stay not; fly, whilst thou art blest and free:
Ne'er see thou man, and let me ne'er see thee.

Exit FLAVIUS. TIMON retires to his cave

*doubt and suspicion have, alas, come too late:
you should have feared betrayal when you were feasting:
men are always suspicious when they are lowest.
What I'm showing, heaven knows, is only love,
duty and loyalty to your noble mind,
taking care of your food and your needs; and
believe me, my most honoured lord,
if there were any benefits which I could get,
either now or in the future, I'd exchange them
for one wish, which would be that you had the power and wealth
to repay me, because you were rich yourself.*

*You see, it's so! You one honest man,
here, take this: through my misery the gods
have sent you treasure. Go, live a rich and happy life;
but on this condition: that you live away from men;
hate them all, curse them all, don't give any
charity to anyone, let the starving flesh fall off
the bone before you help the beggar; give dogs
things that you won't give to men; let the
prisons swallow them,
debts starve them down to nothing; let them be
like dead woods,
and may diseases consume their false blood!
And so farewell, good luck.*

*O, let me stay,
and comfort you, my master.*

*If you hate being cursed,
don't stay here; run, while you are blessed and
free: don't associate with any men, and don't let
me see you again.*

Act 5

SCENE I. The woods. Before Timon's cave.

Enter Poet and Painter; TIMON watching them from his cave

Painter
As I took note of the place, it cannot be far where
he abides.

As far as I remember, his place can't be far from here.

Poet
What's to be thought of him? does the rumour hold
for true, that he's so full of gold?

What should we think of him? Is the rumour true,
that he is stuffed with gold?

Painter
Certain: Alcibiades reports it; Phrynia and
Timandra had gold of him: he likewise enriched poor
straggling soldiers with great quantity: 'tis said
he gave unto his steward a mighty sum.

It's certain: Alcibiades says so; Phrynia and
Timandra had gold from him: he also gave
a large amount to some vagabond soldiers: it's said
he gave a huge sum to his steward.

Poet
Then this breaking of his has been but a try for
his friends.

Then this bankruptcy of his has just been a test
for his friends.

Painter
Nothing else: you shall see him a palm in Athens
again, and flourish with the highest. Therefore
'tis not amiss we tender our loves to him, in this
supposed distress of his: it will show honestly in
us; and is very likely to load our purposes with
what they travail for, if it be a just true report
that goes of his having.

That's all: you'll see him standing tall in Athens
again, and succeeding with the highest. So
it's not a bad thing to offer him our love, in this
faked distress of his: it will make us look loyal;
it will very likely help us to get the rewards
we want, if what they say about him having
a fortune still is true.

Poet
What have you now to present unto him?

What have you got to give to him?

Painter
Nothing at this time but my visitation: only I will
promise him an excellent piece.

Only my company at this time: but I will
promise to do him an excellent painting.

Poet
I must serve him so too, tell him of an intent

I must do the same, tell him of something

113

that's coming toward him.

Painter
Good as the best. Promising is the very air o' the
time: it opens the eyes of expectation:
performance is ever the duller for his act; and,
but in the plainer and simpler kind of people, the
deed of saying is quite out of use. To promise is
most courtly and fashionable: performance is a kind
of will or testament which argues a great sickness
in his judgment that makes it.

TIMON comes from his cave, behind

TIMON
[Aside] Excellent workman! thou canst not paint a
man so bad as is thyself.

Poet
I am thinking what I shall say I have provided for
him: it must be a personating of himself; a satire
against the softness of prosperity, with a discovery
of the infinite flatteries that follow youth and
opulency.

TIMON
[Aside] Must thou needs stand for a villain in
thine own work? wilt thou whip thine own faults in
other men? Do so, I have gold for thee.

Poet
Nay, let's seek him:
Then do we sin against our own estate,
When we may profit meet, and come too late.

Painter
True;

I mean to do for him in the future.

That's as good as the best thing you could give him.
Making promises is what it's all about these days: it gets people expectant. Doing something seems dull; and, except for plain and simple people, doing what one says one will is quite out of fashion. Promising is very posh and fashionable: actually doing is like making a will, a thing which is only done by people who are very sick.

Excellent workman! You can't paint a man as bad as you are yourself.

I am thinking of what I will say I have ready for him: it must be a picture of himself; a satire against the softness of wealth, showing all the flatteries that go with youth and riches.

Do you need to show yourself as a villain in your own work? Will you castigate other men for your own faults? Do so, I have gold for you.

Come on, let's look for him: it would be a sin against our prospects to come too late, when there is a profit to be had.

True;

When the day serves, before black-corner'd night,
Find what thou want'st by free and offer'd light.
Come.

TIMON

[Aside] I'll meet you at the turn. What a god's gold,
That he is worshipp'd in a baser temple
Than where swine feed!
'Tis thou that rigg'st the bark and plough'st the foam,
Settlest admired reverence in a slave:
To thee be worship! and thy saints for aye
Be crown'd with plagues that thee alone obey!
Fit I meet them.

Coming forward

Poet
Hail, worthy Timon!

Painter
Our late noble master!

TIMON
Have I once lived to see two honest men?

Poet
Sir,
Having often of your open bounty tasted,
Hearing you were retired, your friends fall'n off,
Whose thankless natures--O abhorred spirits!--
Not all the whips of heaven are large enough:
What! to you,
Whose star-like nobleness gave life and influence
To their whole being! I am rapt and cannot cover
The monstrous bulk of this ingratitude
With any size of words.

TIMON
Let it go naked, men may see't the better:
You that are honest, by being what you are,

*while the daylight lasts let's find what we're after by the
bright light, before the darkness of night falls.
Come on.*

*I'll intercept you. What a
god gold is,
who is worshipped in a temple
lower than a pigsty!
You're the one who sets the sails and crosses the sea,
makes a slave admire and worship his master:
let you be worshipped! And let your saints
who only follow you be rewarded with plagues!
I should greet them now.*

Greetings, worthy Timon!

Our former noble master!

Have I lived to see two honest men?

*Sir,
having often sampled your great generosity,
hearing you had withdrawn, with your friends abandoning you,
for whose ingratitude--revolting souls that they are!--
There is not enough punishment in heaven:
what! Ingratitude to you,
whose heavenly nobility gave life and meaning
to their whole beings! I'm so moved, I can't begin to put the scale of their ingratitude into words.*

*Just speak plainly, men may see it better:
you who are honest, by being who you are,*

Make them best seen and known.

will show them up for who they are.

Painter
He and myself
Have travail'd in the great shower of your gifts,
And sweetly felt it.

*Him and I
have walked through the shower of your gifts,
which were a sweet rain.*

TIMON
Ay, you are honest men.

Yes, you are honest men.

Painter
We are hither come to offer you our service.

We have come here to offer you our service.

TIMON
Most honest men! Why, how shall I requite
you?
Can you eat roots, and drink cold water? no.

*Most honest men! Why, how shall I repay you?
Can you eat roots, and drink cold water? No.*

Both

What we can do, we'll do, to do you service.

We'll do whatever we can to serve you.

TIMON
Ye're honest men: ye've heard that I have gold;
I am sure you have: speak truth; ye're honest
men.

*You are honest men: you've heard that I have
gold; I'm sure you have heard: tell the truth;
you are honest men.*

Painter
So it is said, my noble lord; but therefore
Came not my friend nor I.

*So they say, my noble lord; but that's not
why my friend nor I came here.*

TIMON
Good honest men! Thou draw'st a counterfeit
Best in all Athens: thou'rt, indeed, the best;
Thou counterfeit'st most lively.

*Good honest men! You can draw a picture
better than anyone in Athens: you're certainly
the best; nobody fakes it better than you.*

Painter
So, so, my lord.

I do it indifferently, my lord.

TIMON
E'en so, sir, as I say. And, for thy fiction,
Why, thy verse swells with stuff so fine and
smooth
That thou art even natural in thine art.
But, for all this, my honest-natured friends,
I must needs say you have a little fault:

*It's just as I say, sir. And as for your inventions,
why, your verse is so puffed up with fine smooth
things
that your art imitates your personality.
But for all this, my honest friends,
I have to say you do have a little fault:*

Marry, 'tis not monstrous in you, neither wish I
You take much pains to mend.

Both
Beseech your honour
To make it known to us.

TIMON
You'll take it ill.

Both
Most thankfully, my lord.

TIMON
Will you, indeed?

Both
Doubt it not, worthy lord.

TIMON
There's never a one of you but trusts a knave,
That mightily deceives you.

Both
Do we, my lord?

TIMON
Ay, and you hear him cog, see him dissemble,
Know his gross patchery, love him, feed him,
Keep in your bosom: yet remain assured
That he's a made-up villain.

Painter
I know none such, my lord.

Poet
Nor I.

TIMON
Look you, I love you well; I'll give you gold,
Rid me these villains from your companies:
Hang them or stab them, drown them in a draught,
Confound them by some course, and come to me,
I'll give you gold enough.

---

mind you, it's not terrible, and I wouldn't want you to take much effort to correct it.

*We beg your honour
to tell us what it is.*

You won't like it.

We would be very grateful to know, my lord.

Would you really?

Don't doubt it, good lord.

*You put your trust in a knave,
who is greatly deceiving you.*

Do we, my lord?

*Yes, and you hear him cheat, see him fake,
know his terrible knavery, love him, feed him,
hold him to your hearts: but you can be sure
that he's a complete villain.*

I don't know anyone like that, my lord.

Nor do I.

*Now look, I like you very much; I'll give you gold,
if you throw these villains out of your company:
hang them or stab them, drown them in a sewer,
defeat them in some way, and come back to me,
I'll give you plenty of gold.*

Both
Name them, my lord, let's know them.

Tell us who they are, my lord, let us know.

TIMON
You that way and you this, but two in company;
Each man apart, all single and alone,
Yet an arch-villain keeps him company.
If where thou art two villains shall not be,
Come not near him. If thou wouldst not reside
But where one villain is, then him abandon.
Hence, pack! there's gold; you came for gold, ye slaves:

You there and you here, just the two of you;
each man standing alone,
but there is a villain with him.
If, where you are, there isn't room for two villains,
don't come near him. If you want to live where there is only one villain, then leave him.
So, be off! Here's gold; you came for gold, you slaves:

To Painter
You have work'd for me; there's payment for you: hence!

[to painter]
you have worked for me; there is payment for you: get out!

To Poet
You are an alchemist; make gold of that.
Out, rascal dogs!

[To poet]
You are an alchemist, make gold out of these stones!

Beats them out, and then retires to his cave

Enter FLAVIUS and two Senators

FLAVIUS
It is in vain that you would speak with Timon;
For he is set so only to himself
That nothing but himself which looks like man
Is friendly with him.

There's no point in trying to speak to Timon;
he is so self absorbed
that the only man he wants to be with
is himself.

First Senator
Bring us to his cave:
It is our part and promise to the Athenians
To speak with Timon.

Take us to his cave:
we have promised the Athenians that we will speak to Timon.

Second Senator
At all times alike
Men are not still the same: 'twas time and griefs
That framed him thus: time, with his fairer hand,
Offering the fortunes of his former days,
The former man may make him. Bring us to him,
And chance it as it may.

Men don't stay the same
at all times: it was a particular circumstance and grief
that made him as he is: time, treating him better,
offering him the fortunes he had in the past,
may change him back to the way he was. Take us to him, and let's see what happens.

FLAVIUS
Here is his cave.
Peace and content be here! Lord Timon!
Timon!
Look out, and speak to friends: the Athenians,
By two of their most reverend senate, greet
thee:
Speak to them, noble Timon.

TIMON comes from his cave

TIMON
Thou sun, that comfort'st, burn! Speak, and
be hang'd:
For each true word, a blister! and each false
Be as cauterizing to the root o' the tongue,
Consuming it with speaking!

First Senator
Worthy Timon,--

TIMON
Of none but such as you, and you of Timon.

First Senator
The senators of Athens greet thee, Timon.

TIMON
I thank them; and would send them back the
plague,
Could I but catch it for them.

First Senator
O, forget
What we are sorry for ourselves in thee.
The senators with one consent of love
Entreat thee back to Athens; who have thought
On special dignities, which vacant lie
For thy best use and wearing.

Second Senator
They confess
Toward thee forgetfulness too general gross:
Which now the public body, which doth seldom
Play the recanter, feeling in itself
A lack of Timon's aid, hath sense withal

Here is his cave.
May peace and happiness be here! Lord Timon!
Timon!
Look out, and speak to friends: the Athenians
send their greetings through two members of
their noble senate:
speak to them, noble Timon.

You sun, that gives comfort, burn! Speak, and
condemn yourselves:
have a blister for every true word! And every
false one should burn you at the root of your
tongues, shrivelling it up as you speak!

Deserving Timon–

I don't deserve anyone but your type, and you
deserve Timon.

The senators of Athens greet you, Timon.

I thank them; I would send them back the
plague,
if I could only catch it for them.

Oh, forget
the wrongs we have done you, which we regret.
The senators are unanimous in their love,
asking you to come back to Athens; they have
invented special honours, which are waiting for
you to assume them.

They admit
that they horribly neglected you:
now the governing body, which doesn't often
take anything back, realises it is missing

Of its own fail, restraining aid to Timon;
And send forth us, to make their sorrow'd
render,
Together with a recompense more fruitful
Than their offence can weigh down by the
dram;
Ay, even such heaps and sums of love and
wealth
As shall to thee blot out what wrongs were
theirs
And write in thee the figures of their love,
Ever to read them thine.

*Timon's help, and at the same time feeling
its own wrong, in declining to help Timon,
have sent us out to offer their apology,
together with compensation which will
outweigh the wrong they have done to you—
yes, such great amounts of love and wealth
that they will wipe out their offences,
and show you the great love they have for you,
which is yours forever.*

TIMON
You witch me in it;
Surprise me to the very brink of tears:
Lend me a fool's heart and a woman's eyes,
And I'll beweep these comforts, worthy
senators.

*You cast your spell over me;
you've almost made me cry:
give me the heart of a fool and a woman's eyes,
and I will weep for joy, good senators.*

First Senator
Therefore, so please thee to return with us
And of our Athens, thine and ours, to take
The captainship, thou shalt be met with thanks,
Allow'd with absolute power and thy good
name
Live with authority: so soon we shall drive
back
Of Alcibiades the approaches wild,
Who, like a boar too savage, doth root up
His country's peace.

*So, please agree to come back with us
and take on the leadership of Athens,
you will be thanked for it, and
given absolute power, and your good name will
be
restored: that way we will soon defeat
the vicious attacks of Alcibiades, who,
like a wild boar, is rooting up
the peace of his country.*

Second Senator
And shakes his threatening sword
Against the walls of Athens.

*And he's threatening the walls of Athens
with his sword.*

First Senator
Therefore, Timon,--

So, Timon—

TIMON
Well, sir, I will; therefore, I will, sir; thus:
If Alcibiades kill my countrymen,
Let Alcibiades know this of Timon,
That Timon cares not. But if he sack fair
Athens,
And take our goodly aged men by the beards,

*Well, sir, I shall tell you what I want:
if Alcibiades kills my countrymen,
tell Alcibiades this from Timon,
that Timon doesn't care. But if he sacks lovely
Athens,
and takes our good old men by the beards,*

120

Giving our holy virgins to the stain
Of contumelious, beastly, mad-brain'd war,
Then let him know, and tell him Timon speaks it,
In pity of our aged and our youth,
I cannot choose but tell him, that I care not,
And let him take't at worst; for their knives care not,
While you have throats to answer: for myself,
There's not a whittle in the unruly camp
But I do prize it at my love before
The reverend'st throat in Athens. So I leave you
To the protection of the prosperous gods,
As thieves to keepers.

sacrifices our holy virgins to the stain of arrogant, beastly, insane war, then let him know, and tell him Timon says it, out of pity for our old people and youths, that's all I can tell him, is that I don't care, and let him interpret that whichever way he likes; don't worry about their knives while you still have throats to give them. For myself, there's not a single soldier in the rebel camp that I don't value more than the most exalted person in Athens. So I leave you in the protection of the favourable gods, as I would leave thieves with their jailers.

FLAVIUS
Stay not, all's in vain.

Don't stay here, you're wasting your time.

TIMON
Why, I was writing of my epitaph;
it will be seen to-morrow: my long sickness
Of health and living now begins to mend,
And nothing brings me all things. Go, live still;
Be Alcibiades your plague, you his,
And last so long enough!

Why, I was writing my epitaph; you will see it tomorrow: my long illness of being healthy and alive is beginning to be cured, and oblivion is bringing me everything. Go, stay alive; May Alcibiades torture you, you him, and both of you live long in suffering.

First Senator
We speak in vain.

Our speech was useless.

TIMON
But yet I love my country, and am not
One that rejoices in the common wreck,
As common bruit doth put it.

But I still love my country, and I'm not one of those who rejoices at its downfall, as rumour has it.

First Senator
That's well spoke.

That's well said.

TIMON
Commend me to my loving countrymen,--

Give my loving countrymen my best wishes—

First Senator
These words become your lips as they pass thorough them.

These words glorify your lips as they pass through them.

Second Senator
And enter in our ears like great triumphers

And they sound as sweet to us as the applause

In their applauding gates.

the crowd gives to triumphant generals.

TIMON
Commend me to them,
And tell them that, to ease them of their griefs,
Their fears of hostile strokes, their aches,
losses,
Their pangs of love, with other incident throes
That nature's fragile vessel doth sustain
In life's uncertain voyage, I will some kindness
do them:
I'll teach them to prevent wild Alcibiades'
wrath.

Give them my greetings,
and tell them that, to alleviate their worries,
their fear of hostile blows, their aches, losses,
their pangs of love, and the other incidental
blows
that nature's fragile ship suffers
in the uncertain voyage of life, I will do them a
favour:
I'll tell them how to escape the anger of wild
Alcibiades.

First Senator
I like this well; he will return again.

I like this; he will come back.

TIMON
I have a tree, which grows here in my close,
That mine own use invites me to cut down,
And shortly must I fell it: tell my friends,
Tell Athens, in the sequence of degree
From high to low throughout, that whoso please
To stop affliction, let him take his haste,
Come hither, ere my tree hath felt the axe,
And hang himself. I pray you, do my greeting.

I have a tree which grows close by here,
which I must cut down for my own needs,
I will do it shortly: tell my friends,
Tel Athens, all of them from the
highest to the lowest, that whoever wants
to end the horror, let him hurry here,
before I've cut down the tree,
and hang himself from it. Please pass this on.

FLAVIUS
Trouble him no further; thus you still shall find
him.

Don't bother him any more; he'll always be like
this.

TIMON
Come not to me again: but say to Athens,
Timon hath made his everlasting mansion
Upon the beached verge of the salt flood;
Who once a day with his embossed froth
The turbulent surge shall cover: thither come,
And let my grave-stone be your oracle.
Lips, let sour words go by and language end:
What is amiss plague and infection mend!
Graves only be men's works and death their
gain!
Sun, hide thy beams! Timon hath done his
reign.

Don't come back to me: but say to Athens,
Timon has made his eternal home
on the sandy edge of the sea;
once a day he shall be covered
by the foaming tide: come there,
visit my gravestone for advice.
Lips, speak these sour words and then let
talking finish:
let plague and infection cure what is wrong!
Let graves be the only works men make, and
death their profit!
Sun, hide your beams! Timon has finished.

Retires to his cave

First Senator

His discontents are unremoveably
Coupled to nature.

*His anger is irrevocably
ingrained in his nature.*

Second Senator

Our hope in him is dead: let us return,
And strain what other means is left unto us
In our dear peril.

*We have no more hope in him: let's go back,
and do whatever other things we have left
to save us from our danger.*

First Senator

It requires swift foot.

We shall have to hurry.

Exeunt

SCENE II. Before the walls of Athens.

Enter two Senators and a Messenger

First Senator
Thou hast painfully discover'd: are his files
As full as thy report?

This news of yours is painful: are his forces as large as you say?

Messenger
I have spoke the least:
Besides, his expedition promises
Present approach.

That's the lowest estimate: besides, he's coming so quickly that he will be here almost immediately.

Second Senator
We stand much hazard, if they bring not
Timon.

We are in great danger, if they don't bring Timon back.

Messenger
I met a courier, one mine ancient friend;
Whom, though in general part we were
opposed,
Yet our old love made a particular force,
And made us speak like friends: this man was
riding
From Alcibiades to Timon's cave,
With letters of entreaty, which imported
His fellowship i' the cause against your city,
In part for his sake moved.

I met a messenger, an old friend of mine; although we are fighting on different sides our old liking for each other was strong, and we spoke like friends: this man was riding from Alcibiades to Timon's cave, with letters asking him to join forces against your city, as the expedition was begun partly for his sake.

First Senator
Here come our brothers.

Here come our brothers.

Enter the Senators from TIMON

Third Senator
No talk of Timon, nothing of him expect.
The enemies' drum is heard, and fearful
scouring
Doth choke the air with dust: in, and prepare:
Ours is the fall, I fear; our foes the snare.

Don't talk about Timon, don't expect anything from him. The drums of the enemy have been heard, and the terrifying preparations are filling the air with dust: go in, and prepare: I fear we are going to succumb to our enemy's plans.

Exeunt

SCENE III. The woods. Timon's cave, and a rude tomb seen.

Enter a Soldier, seeking TIMON

Soldier

By all description this should be the place.
Who's here? speak, ho! No answer! What is
this?
"Timon is dead, who hath outstretch'd his span:
Some beast read this; there does not live a
man."
Dead, sure; and this his grave. What's on this
tomb
I cannot read; the character I'll take with wax:
Our captain hath in every figure skill,
An aged interpreter, though young in days:
Before proud Athens he's set down by this,
Whose fall the mark of his ambition is.

Exit

From everything I was told this should be the
place. Who's here? Hello! No answer! What is
this?
"Timon is dead, having outlived his time:
some animal can read this; no man lives here."
He's dead, for certain; this is his grave. I can't
read what's on this tomb; I'll take an
impression of the inscription with wax:
our captain knows all languages,
an experienced interpreter, even though he's
young:
he's already pitched his tents in front of proud
Athens, the fall of which is his goal.

SCENE IV. Before the walls of Athens.

Trumpets sound. Enter ALCIBIADES with his powers

ALCIBIADES
Sound to this coward and lascivious town
Our terrible approach.

A parley sounded

Enter Senators on the walls

Till now you have gone on and fill'd the time
With all licentious measure, making your wills
The scope of justice; till now myself and such
As slept within the shadow of your power
Hav e wander'd with our traversed arms and
breathed
Our sufferance vainly: now the time is flush,
When crouching marrow in the bearer strong
Cries of itself 'No more:' now breathless wrong
Shall sit and pant in your great chairs of ease,
And pursy insolence shall break his wind
With fear and horrid flight.

First Senator
Noble and young,
When thy first griefs were but a mere conceit,
Ere thou hadst power or we had cause of fear,
We sent to thee, to give thy rages balm,
To wipe out our ingratitude with loves
Above their quantity.

Second Senator
So did we woo
Transformed Timon to our city's love
By humble message and by promised means:
We were not all unkind, nor all descrve
The common stroke of war.

First Senator
These walls of ours
Were not erected by their hands from whom

You have received your griefs; nor are they
such
That these great towers, trophies and schools

126

Notify this cowardly and lustful town
of our terrifying approach.

Until now you have carried on and filled your
time with every sort of depraved behaviour,
making justice the servant of your desires; until
now myself and those who dwelt in the shadow
of your power have wandered with our swords
sheathed and complained in vain: now the time
is ripe, when the courage rises inside a man
and cries out, 'No more': now the breathless
wronged ones shall sit and rest in your great
luxurious thrones,
while you burst your lungs
with fear and flight.

Noble young man,
when you had only thoughts of these actions,
before you had power or we had reason to be
afraid, we sent you messages to address your
grievances, offering to compensate you for our
ingratitude with honours
greater than the harm we had done you.

In the same way we tried
to bring Timon back into the fold,
with humble messages and promised rewards:
not all of us were unkind, and not all of us
deserve
to suffer the indiscriminate blows of war.

These walls of ours
were not built by the hands of those who
have harmed you; nor should all
these great towers, monuments and public
buildings

should fall
For private faults in them.

fall because of
the individual faults of those people.

Second Senator
Nor are they living
Who were the motives that you first went out;
Shame that they wanted cunning, in excess
Hath broke their hearts. March, noble lord,
Into our city with thy banners spread:
By decimation, and a tithed death--
If thy revenges hunger for that food
Which nature loathes--take thou the destined
tenth,
And by the hazard of the spotted die
Let die the spotted.

Nor are the ones who first drove you away
still living;
ashamed that they couldn't carry through their
plans, their hearts have been broken. March,
noble lord,
into our city with your banners unfurled:
kill one person in every ten,
if your revenge is hungry for that unnatural
reward, take the allocated tenth
and let the spotted dice decide which of those
who are spotted with guilt should die.

First Senator
All have not offended;
For those that were, it is not square to take
On those that are, revenges: crimes, like lands,
Are not inherited. Then, dear countryman,
Bring in thy ranks, but leave without thy rage:
Spare thy Athenian cradle and those kin
Which in the bluster of thy wrath must fall
With those that have offended: like a shepherd,
Approach the fold and cull the infected forth,
But kill not all together.

Not everyone has injured you;
it is not fair to take revenge on those who didn't
to punish those who did: crimes are not
inherited like property. So, dear countryman,
bring in your forces, but leave your anger
outside: Spare the city of your birth and your
brothers who must fall in the storm of your
anger alongside those who have injured you:
like a shepherd, come to the flock and kill the
infected ones, but don't slaughter them all.

Second Senator
What thou wilt,
Thou rather shalt enforce it with thy smile
Than hew to't with thy sword.

Whatever you want,
you can get it with your smile,
you don't have to cut it out with your sword.

First Senator
Set but thy foot
Against our rampired gates, and they shall ope;
So thou wilt send thy gentle heart before,
To say thou'lt enter friendly.

Just nudge our reinforced gates
with your foot, and they shall open;
provided that you send a kind message
in advance, to say you will come in peace.

Second Senator
Throw thy glove,
Or any token of thine honour else,
That thou wilt use the wars as thy redress
And not as our confusion, all thy powers
Shall make their harbour in our town, till we
Have seal'd thy full desire.

Throw down your glove,
or any other pledge of your honour,
to show you will use the wars to get your
compensation, not to destroy us, all your forces
shall have safe lodgings in our town, until we
have given you everything you want.

ALCIBIADES
Then there's my glove;
Descend, and open your uncharged ports:
Those enemies of Timon's and mine own
Whom you yourselves shall set out for reproof
Fall and no more: and, to atone your fears
With my more noble meaning, not a man
Shall pass his quarter, or offend the stream
Of regular justice in your city's bounds,
But shall be render'd to your public laws
At heaviest answer.

Then here's my glove;
come down, and open your undamaged doors:
the enemies of Timon and of me,
whom you yourselves admitted deserve
punishment, shall die and no others: and, to
calm your fears and show my noble purpose, no
man will stray from barracks, or offend against
the laws of the city, without being
handed over to your civil courts
for the greatest punishment you can give.

Both
'Tis most nobly spoken.

That is very nobly said.

ALCIBIADES
Descend, and keep your words.

Come down, and keep your word.

The Senators descend, and open the gates

Enter Soldier

Soldier
My noble general, Timon is dead;
Entomb'd upon the very hem o' the sea;
And on his grave-stone this insculpture, which
With wax I brought away, whose soft
impression
Interprets for my poor ignorance.

My noble general, Timon is dead;
his tomb is on the edge of the sea;
this inscription was on his gravestone, which
I made an impression of in wax,
which makes up for my inability to read it.

ALCIBIADES
[Rcads the epitaph] 'Here lies a
wretched corse, of wretched soul bereft:
Seek not my name: a plague consume you
wicked
caitiffs left!
Here lie I, Timon; who, alive, all living men did
hate:
Pass by and curse thy fill, but pass and stay
not here thy gait.'
These well express in thee thy latter spirits:
Though thou abhorr'dst in us our human griefs,
Scorn'dst our brain's flow and those our
droplets which
From niggard nature fall, yet rich conceit

"Here lies a
wretched corpse, whose wretched soul has left
it: don't look for my name: may a plague
overwhelm you
wicked rascals left!
Here lies Timon, who all living men hated when
he was alive:
pass by and curse all you want, but keep going,
don't stop here."
These words show your last mood well:
although you despised our human griefs,
hated the tiny droplets of tears which fell
from parsimonious nature, your rich
imagination

129

Taught thee to make vast Neptune weep for aye
On thy low grave, on faults forgiven. Dead
Is noble Timon: of whose memory
Hereafter more. Bring me into your city,
And I will use the olive with my sword,
Make war breed peace, make peace stint war, make each
Prescribe to other as each other's leech.
Let our drums strike.

Exeunt

showed you how to make the great ocean weep for you at your low grave, asking for forgiveness. Noble Timon is dead: we shall speak about him more later. Bring me into your city, and I will show mercy while still being strong, let war bring peace, let peace stop war, make each one
work for the good of each, like doctors treating each other. Strike up the drums.

89485548R00073

Made in the USA
San Bernardino, CA
26 September 2018